2020 THE LEAP OF FAITH:
THE DAWNING OF A NEW WORLD

"Gahl Sasson take the complicated task of living well and gives it grace, intelligence and purpose. You will be engaged and prepared for the year ahead and enchanted by the masterful storytelling of Gahl Sasson. For those who live by the planets, this book is full of detailed navigation and powerful advice. For those who just want to know how to do their best, this reads like a book of mythology with grounded, practical advice."

Laura Day, bestselling author of *The Circle* and *Practical Intuition.*

about author

Gahl Sasson is an established author and has been teaching workshops on Storytelling, Kabbalah, Astrology, and Mysticism around the globe for over 20 years. His first book, *A Wish Can Change Your Life*, has been translated into over eight languages and is endorsed by HH the 14th Dalai Lama. His latest work, *Cosmic Navigator*, is the essential reference guide to understanding your astrological makeup. He is a contributor to the Huffington Post, and Astrology.com, and has been named by W Magazine as one of "Los Angeles' Best Astrologer."

Gahl was also chosen by Asia Spa Magazine as one of the 10 leading health practitioners in the world. His encyclopedic knowledge and charismatic presence have also made him a sought-after guest speaker. He is a guest lecturer at USC, Tel Aviv University, and teaches at Esalen, Omega Institute, University of Judaism, and the Open Center in NYC. He has appeared on CNN, ABC News, KTLA-TV Los Angeles to name a few. In 2017 his academic article, *Symbolic Meaning of Names in the Bible* was published by the Journal of Storytelling, Self, & Society. He currently resides in Los Angeles, but gives seminars and workshops regularly in USA, Argentina, France, Germany, Canada, Mexico, Russia, Lithuania, UK, Hong Kong, Spain, Israel, Singapore, Turkey, Israel, Bulgaria, and Switzerland. His web site is www.CosmicNavigator.com

Special thanks to Kibea Publishing for designing the book and to Michael Davis' and Mary Plumb's editing skills. Photo Credits: Alex Richardson and Abbas Suliman.

GAHL EDEN SASSON

The Astrology of 2020

GAHL E. SASSON

KIBEA

T H E   A S T R O L O G Y   O F

2020

The Leap of Faith: The Dawning of a New World

For decades, astrologers and stargazers around the world looked forward as well as dreaded the arrival of the year 2020. While some prophesized disaster (coming from Greek: *dis-aster*, against the stars), others identified the year as the dawning of a new era. I tend to follow the advice of the Lord Buddha, a sensible Taurus with moon in Scorpio, who emphasized the importance of walking the middle path: 2020 is a dreadful year that can potentially set humanity into a new eon. Another counsel to heed comes from the Sufis, who suggested that, fearing thieves at night, one should trust in Allah, but tie the camels first. We should trust the stars, but we should also prepare for the stories they will luster upon us.

What music do the spheres wish to play for us in the year ahead? What synchronized stories do the constellations wish us to enact? What can we expect from a year whose numerology, 4 and 22, suggests both bereavement and mastery over the mysteries of life? What can we make of the fact that we have six eclipses instead of the usual four and that one of them falls right on the Summer Solstice and another smack on the birthday of the USA?

What does it mean to have a "Great Conjunction" of Jupiter and Saturn right on the Winter Solstice, which for the first time since early 1800s, has shifted from earth signs to air signs? What does it mean that Mercury retrogrades while Venus and Mars also appear to orbit backward?

And, most importantly, what should we do about that rare conjunction of Saturn (Lord Karma) and Pluto (Lord of Death)? What is 2020 planning for us considering that the last few times this conjunction took place, the AIDS epidemic broke out, the Cold War started, and World War I begun?

But don't worry. I am a middle path guy, remember? I just gave you the overture of the celestial symphony called Opus 2020. So please don't toss the book away or lose hope. I truly believe that in 2020 we can open a new doc on our cosmic operating system and explore the next chapter in our ever-evolutionary history as *Homo sapiens*. The 2020 triple conjunction: Pluto with Saturn, Saturn with Jupiter, and Pluto with Jupiter, promises a new beginning, a way to break old patterns. The word "patterns" comes from Old French, "something serving as a model," hence *patron*, or boss. I guess the old French thought a boss should serve as a good model. This year, we can free ourselves from old patrons, breaking the shackles of the patriarchal "strong man" paradigm, whether these so-called "strong men" are inside of us or manifest collectively outside.

In Chinese Astrology, 2020 is the Year of the Metal Rat, the first of the animal wheel, the initiator of a new cycle. In addition, Jupiter and Saturn's grand alignment right on the Winter Solstice, the ancient birthday of the gods of light, takes place in Aquarius, the sign of altruism, humanity, and hope.

Perhaps this year will be the true dawning of the Age of Aquarius and, with the help of our positive intentions, we can herald a new age of enlightenment, freedom, and equality.

I wish you a transformative and meaningful year full of health, magic, and synchronicities.

With love from the shores of the Aegean, a sea that launched a thousand myths . . .

Summer Solstice, 2019
Gahl

GENERAL GUIDES:
RETROGRADE & STATIONARY PLANETS

Mercury

• Feb 16 – March 10: Pisces, Feb 16 to March 4; Aquarius, March 4 to 10.
• June 18 – July 12: Cancer.
• Oct 13 – Nov 4: Scorpio, Oct 13 to Oct 27; Libra, Oct 27 to Nov 4.

Do not: sign documents, start projects, publish.
Do: backup computers, edit, revisit old projects.

Venus

• May 13 – June 25: Gemini.

Do not: start new relationships, make big purchases, sign partnership agreements.
Do: reevaluate your values and the way you make money, redo old contracts.

Mars

- Sep 9 – Nov 14: Aries.

Do not: buy big machinery, start wars or lawsuits, undergo surgeries (unless urgent), start big campaigns, start intimate relationships.

Do: change exercise routines, change the way you work, reexamine your passion and sexuality.

SOLAR AND LUNAR ECLIPSES IN 2020

Events quicken and manifest faster.
Lunar eclipse: emotional, end of processes.
Solar eclipse: call for action, new beginnings.

- **Jan 10/11** – Cancer Lunar penumbra eclipse.
- **June 5/6** – Sagittarius Lunar penumbral eclipse.
- **June 21** – Cancer Solar annular eclipse.
- **July 4/5** – Capricorn Lunar penumbral eclipse.
- **Nov 29/30** – Gemini Lunar penumbral eclipse.
- **Dec 14** – Sagittarius total Solar eclipse

.

SPECIAL GUESTS STARS:
Important Days to Notice

- **Jan 10:** Lunar eclipse.
- **Jan 12:** Pluto and Saturn conjunction (first since 1982). See chapter below.
- **Jan 25:** New Moon in Aquarius: Chinese New Year of the Metal Rat.
- **Jan 25 – 29:** Venus and Neptune conjunct. Romance!
- **Jan 21 – Jan 31:** First Venus and Mars square. Challenges in relationships.
- **Feb 8 – 11:** Venus, Chiron, and Lilith conjunct in Aries. Wounds from relationships.
- **Feb 16 – March 10:** Mercury retrograde in Pisces. Relapses, confusion, misunderstandings.
- **Feb 18 – Feb 21:** Stellium in Capricorn: Moon, Mars, Jupiter, Pluto, Saturn, and Pallas. Slow down, lessons in patience.
- **March 5 – March 10:** Venus conjunct Uranus. Unpredictable love. Financial rollercoaster.
- **March 22 – July 1:** Saturn in Aquarius (first time since 1991). Change in political wind.
- **March 25 – 31:** Trine between Venus and Pluto, Mars, Jupiter. Great for art and love.
- **April 4 – May 10:** Trine between Mars and Venus. Great for love, harmony, creativity.
- **March 21 – April 10:** First conjunction Jupiter and Pluto. Exact on April 5. Power and flow.
- **May 13 – June 25:** Venus retrograde in Gemini. Exes reappear, reevaluation of finances & values.

- **May 14 – Sep 13:** Jupiter retrograde. Gifts held in a cosmic saving account until mid-Sep.
- **May 31 – June 6:** Mars square Venus retrograde. Strife and discord in relationships.
- **June 5:** Lunar eclipse. Things moving faster. Truth versus lies.
- **June 7 – June 16:** Mars and Neptune conjunct. Watch your immune system and be careful of deceptions.
- **June 18 – July 12:** Mercury retrograde in Cancer. Miscommunications at home.
- **June 21:** Solar eclipse right on the solstice while Venus and Mercury are retrograde. INTENSE!
- **June 28 – Jan 6, 2021:** Mars, god of war, in Aries, sign of war.
- **June 16 – July 14:** Second conjunction Jupiter and Pluto. Exact on June 30.
- **July 1 – Dec 16:** Saturn returns to Capricorn. Change in political and financial structures.
- **July 5:** Lunar eclipse. Home versus career.
- **July 7 – 17:** Mars conjunct Chiron. Injuries, wounds, insecurities.
- **July 8 – 27:** Mars and Mercury square. Challenges in relationships and partnerships, overspending. Exact July 8 & 27.
- **July 27 – Oct 20:** Mars squares Pluto and Saturn. Aggression, war, power struggles.
- **August 1 – August 5:** North Node conjunct Venus. Meetings with like-minded people, artists.
- **Sep 1 – Sep 4:** Mars Venus square. Challenges in love.
- **Sep 9 – Nov 14:** Mars retro in Aries. Bad for surgeries, campaigning, and starting big projects.

- **Oct 13 – Nov 3:** Mercury retro in Scorpio. Deadly misunderstandings.
- **Oct 15 – 22:** Venus opposite Neptune. Addictions, dependency, disillusionment in relationships.
- **Oct 31 – Nov 16:** Third conjunction Jupiter and Pluto. Exact on Nov 12.
- **Nov 30:** Lunar eclipse. Lies versus truth.
- **Dec 14:** Solar eclipse. New beginning for travel, education, revelation of truth.
- **Dec 19:** Jupiter moves to Aquarius for a year. Liberal values and globalization return.
- **Dec 21:** Jupiter and Saturn conjunction in Aquarius (first since 2000). Dawning of a new era.

Part I

Introduction to Cosmic Trends

Synchronicities:
As Above, So Below

"Astrology represents the sum of all the
psychological knowledge of antiquity"
Carl G. Jung

All mystical traditions I have thus far encountered proclaim that all is one and one is all. They agree that creation and creator are one. Astrology is based on this premise and uses the idea of oneness to argue that, since everything is connected, the planetary movement in the heavens are corelated, synchronized, and therefore linked to life on earth.

For thousands of years, wise men and women from different continents and diverse religions empirically traced, identified, and analyzed the connections between the trajectories of heavenly bodies and the drama taking place on earth. Through their observations and keen intellect, they managed to repeatedly validate the alchemical axiom of "As Above, So Below." They managed to connect the complex orbits and cycles above with what happens on our planet below to the point that predictions of the future events were possible.

Every child knows that in winter it is cold and summer it is hot, even without knowing that the reason for the seasons is the 23-degree tilt of the earth.

The preschooler can predict, based on her experiences, that in winter we will wear coats and use umbrellas. Astrology was born out of the need to understand cycles on earth. When would the rivers flood? When should we plant or harvest? It was the observation of the moon's cycles that taught our female ancestors how to predict and time their menstruation cycles. Astrology helped us survive and get to this stage of evolution and astrology can also help you reach the next level of your spiritual development.

It is not a coincidence that the man who coined the word "synchronicity," also studied astrology. In a letter to Freud, Carl G. Jung writes that his "evenings are taken up very largely with the study of astrology." He further argues that astrology and its study of archetypes and signs are "the sum of all the psychological knowledge of antiquity." Jung developed his theories of the collective unconscious and archetypes at the same time that he recognized the importance of synchronicities. He believed that the synchronicities we experience in life are proof of the interconnectedness of existence. In astrology, these archetypes, or ideals, as Plato would have called them, are found in the zodiac signs and planets. Astrology is the study of the signature of all things: the synchronized tango between the planets and our lives. There is no cause and effect in synchronicity, but only correlation. When the six eclipses take place in 2020, they do not *cause* life to quicken, but are signs or omens that tell us "Now, things will move fast. Hold on!"

When Mercury retrogrades, he does not make you send an email with an incriminating trail at the bottom. He just informs us that, while he walks backwards, statistically speaking, we experience communication glitches and misunderstandings. Planets do not cause anything to happen, they are the messengers, not the message.

In Genesis 1:14, on the fourth day of creation, God says, "Let there be lights in the firmament of the heaven to divide the day from the night; and let them be for *signs*, and for seasons, and for days, and years." Astrology's long mission was, is, and shall always be to provide an interpretation of these signs and seasons.

Zeitgeist Wonderland – *The Spirit of the Time*

The great German philosopher, Georg Hegel (1770 – 1831), argued that "no man can surpass his own time, for the spirit of his time is also his own spirit." Even though he never used the word, his philosophy was summed up by the idea of *Zeitgeist*, from the German words, *Zeit*, meaning "time," and *Geist*, meaning "spirit." Astrology is the best device to capture the "spirit of the time" using the outer planets, Uranus, Neptune, and Pluto, whose long orbits provide insight into larger periods of time. In 2020, all these planets are pointing at significant changes in the spirit of the time. One may argue that, in 2020, an era dies and a new one is born. Therefore, we can expect a change in "the spirit of the time," which can manifest in art, economy, and politics.

The reason why I love astrology is because it is a multidisciplinary art that requires the practitioner to delve into history, mythology, philosophy, psychology, politics, and storytelling, as well as demanding a great deal of creativity and imagination.

To understand what is happening right now or in the next few years, we must trace, understand, and analyze prior similar planetary alignments and cycles and study what occurred on earth at that time. In other words, we must identify past synchronicities in order to understand the spirit of the time.

However, as with any other skill, from parenting to business, trading to art, astrology is a blend of knowledge and intuition. The best results of any task unfold when we utilize both of our brain hemispheres. You will receive a great deal of information about the trends, zeitgeist, and synchronicities of 2020, but it will be up to your intuition to relate it to your life and make the best of it.

Alice of Wonderland, who I have always regarded as a typical Piscean, has an interesting conversation with the White Queen (Lewis Carroll, *Through the Looking Glass*). Alice sensibly says, that she can only remember things that happened in the past. The White Queen, flabbergasted, replies that it is a "poor sort of memory that only works backwards." The White Queen suggests Alice should try remembering things that happened in the future. Alice asks the White Queen, "What sort of things do you remember best?" and the queen nonchalantly replies, "Oh, things that happened the week after next."

It was Einstein, the high school dropout Piscean, who, after realizing time and space are bent, concluded that time is an illusion. Put together, the mystical imaginative clan of Pisces advocates that we should heed the suggestions of the White Queen and develop the skill of remembering the future. Astrology for thousands of years has been training us to do precisely that.

Let us approach this year as a Wonder Year, a year where we can remember things to come, a year where we can imagine and visualize what we want to happen, a year where we design our destiny.

However, just as a landscape designer must envision the garden he wants to plant based on the climate zone, so do we need to know the planetary climate of 2020 to be able to visualize what we want to grow in the next 12 months.

The Stories of 2020

Numbers Tell Stories

Pythagoras and his followers are credited with the development of what we call today numerology, the belief that numbers are not only designed to *count* objects but also to *account* for stories. In numerology, numbers, just like the astrological signs, are vessels of archetypes. In numerology, the year 2020 is reduced to two numbers: 22 as well as 4 (2+0+2+0=4). 22 is a Master Number and below I will explain what it means for the year ahead. But since the number 2020 is made out of the digits 2 and 0, it is important to understand their symbolic significance first.

The number 2 symbolizes relationships, duality, reflection, and, since it is the closest number to 1 (and oneness) that is not 1, it has the best view of number 1 and the unity it represents. Therefore, in Kabbalah, 2 is associated with Sofia, the sphere "Wisdom" in the Tree of Life. Wisdom is the ability to see oneness in everything you meet. That is why the Sufi say that a wise man or women is someone who sees God (oneness) in everyone they meet. The number 2 symbolizes the meeting of 1 with oneself, thus endorsing self-awareness and meditation.

The digit 0, a latecomer to the number gang, was first used in India in the 7th century and brought to the West by Arab voyagers. Zero was, of course, outlawed and excommunicated for a while, but mathematicians as well as merchants found it to be very efficient in calculation and thus it survived. Zero's archetype is neither masculine (like 1) nor feminine (like 2). By default, it has *zero* gender. The best depiction of zero comes from the tarot as well as playing cards. The *Joker* or *Fool* is associated with the archetype of zero. The word "fool" comes from Latin *follis*, air, nothingness, therefore, full of potential.

In Kabbalah, this primordial emptiness is called *Ain* and, in Buddhism, *Sunyata*. In countless other traditions, creation emerges *ex nihilo*, out of emptiness, out of nothing. That is why the Joker in the playing cards can be replaced by any card of the deck. The Fool is none of the cards, therefore all of them. The Fool in the tarot symbolizes the leap of faith, a jump across the abyss, a need to take the plunge and trust! With so many zeros in 2020, the mantra of the year is: NO FEAR! Remember, that was also the mantra of 2000, when the Y2K madness was driving people crazy with fear.

Since in 2020 we have *two* 0s and *two* 2s, we are encouraged by our digital friends to take a leap of faith into our relationships or whatever it is in our lives that serves as our mirrors.

These mirrors of oneness could be anything from a lover, a partner in work, a child, art, literature, meditation, or a hobby.

2020 is a good year to explore new avenues of collaboration, peaceful solutions, diplomacy, justice, fairness, equality, and love, since all these aspects of life are represented by the number 2. Like the Fool, we should assume a "child mind" and reconnect to youthful naiveté, exploring anew the intoxicating uplifting feeling of love and enthusiasm.

In Numerology, 2020 is first reduced to 22, which, as was mentioned, is a Master Number, like 11 and 33, and therefore, traditionally, should not be further reduced to 4. The Master Number 22 is also called *Master Builder* and in some circles is associated with the idea of twin-flames. But first, let's take a closer look at the story of number 4, since with a 2020 triple conjunction of Pluto, Saturn, and Jupiter along with Mars, the planet of war, revenging through Aries, the fire cardinal sign, for six months, we should explore the darker aspects of the number.

In China, Japan, Hong Kong, Taiwan, and Korea, people will go to great length to avoid an encounter of the 4th kind. In many buildings, just like 13 in the West (which also adds to 4), the 4th floor does not exist. This tetraphobia derives from the fact that the word for 4 *sì* is homophonous with the word "death." In Feng-Shui, one is highly encouraged to avoid clusters of 4, for example, four lucky bamboos in one jar, or four pillows on a sofa, etc.

Since there are over 1.5 billion people who consider 4 unlucky and inauspicious, we can deduce that even if it would have been a good number in another tradition, its shadow is cast far and long.

However, the story of 4 is also filled with strife in the West through its association to the square. In Hebrew, *yashar* is the word for "fight," and is also used to describe a right angle or 90 degrees, corresponding to a square. In English, when two people prepare to fight, they square-off. Being "a square" is being a bore, conventional, out-of-date, and uninteresting. In astrology, when two planets form a square, meaning they are located in the chart 90 degrees apart, they bring out the worst of each other.

For example, in July 2020, Mars and Venus are squaring, which is synchronized with impulsiveness and aggression (Mars) in relationships or finance (Venus). The number 4 symbolizes structure, formidability, an impenetrable fortress.

For example, the 4 of Disks in the *tarot* deck is called *Power* and astrologically is associated with the Sun in Capricorn. This year, we have a rare alignment of Pluto (since 2008), Saturn (since 2017), South Node (since 2018), and Jupiter (Since 2019) in Capricorn. Indeed, 2020 is a year of power struggles where the forces of change will try to breach the formidable structure of fear, nationalism, and other such squares.

Ok, you might think, so what do I do with this information? Death, fights, squares, immovable situations?

Well, I think that there is a reason why magic, defined as creating something out of nothing, uses spells (words that transform) as well as symbols.

You can work with symbols by shifting them around. For example, a pentagram is a symbol of protection. When turned upside down, it becomes a symbol of ignorance. My suggestion is to shift the square 45 degrees, creating a diamond:

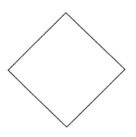

Diamonds are a solid form of the element, carbon, essentially coal that has been subjected to immense pressure over a long period of time. Diamonds are considered the strongest natural material on the planet, symbolizing endurance and experience gained through hard life lessons. Diamonds cut through glass, puncturing illusions and, in crystal healing, are considered enhancers or amplifiers of energy and intentions. Since so many planets are in Capricorn, the sign of earth and time, let us work with diamonds as an anchor or a capsule of space and time to help us through the squareness of the 2020. I am not suggesting buying a diamond. The glittering rock has been kidnapped by square-minded people who manipulate their prices for no reason.

I simply recommend working with diamonds, not with your seeing eyes, but with your all-seeing third eye. Imagine, visualize, and conjure a mega-diamond and work with it in your meditation this year. An example for a diamond meditation is found at the end of this section.

Master Builder Catch-22

In 1961, Joseph Heller published his war story, *Catch-22*. Since then, it became a term that expresses a paradoxical dilemma, wherein the attempt to escape makes escape impossible. Of course, this is not a new concept. Being human is, by default, a catch-22 situation. The Greek tragedies are all catch-22 stories. That is why they usually end with everyone dead at the last act. In Heller's story, the logic loop or catch-22 describes a situation where a soldier who wants to get out of combat duty cannot proclaim himself insane since it is sane to try to avoid deadly situation. From the book:

Yossarian looked at him soberly and tried another approach. "Is Orr crazy?"

"He sure is," Doc Daneeka said.

"Can you ground him?"

"I sure can. But first he has to ask me to. That's part of the rule."

"Then why doesn't he ask you to?"

"Because he's crazy," Doc Daneeka said. "He has to be crazy to keep flying combat missions after all the close calls he's had. Sure, I can ground Orr. But first he has to ask me to."

"That's all he has to do to be grounded?"

"That's all. Let him ask me."

"And then you can ground him?" Yossarian asked.

"No. Then I can't ground him."

"You mean there's a catch?"

"Sure there's a catch," Doc Daneeka replied. "Catch-22. Anyone who wants to get out of combat duty isn't really crazy."

2020 is a catch-22. It is a Master Builder year, since its numerology is 22, a great number for building a new world order and starting a new era. 22 is associated with the Fool, the first card that contains all the rest of the 22 Major Arcana within it. These cards are also associated with the 22 Hebrew letters, which in Kabbalah are the building blocks the creator used to masterfully build the cosmos. Great! But it is also a 4, associated with death, fear, keeping the status-quo, scarce resource mentality, the more-for-you-means-less-for-me attitude. So, in 2020, should we stay low and do time? Mark lines for every day on the wall and wait for the year to be over? Or should we go out there and be a master builder even if what we build could be destroyed by the number 4?

The number 4 and its acolytes do not want a new order. They clench their grip on the past. They only want to masterfully build walls, detention centers, and borders. They insist climate is not changing and that coal is clean energy!

Four is associated with maturity, the kind of energy that encourages older people to decide the future even though they will die soon, while younger people, who actually have a future, are not being heard.

Pluto (power) and Saturn (structure) are in Capricorn (status quo), while the North Node, the sign of where we are headed, is in the opposite sign of Cancer (compassion and unconditional love). We are trapped in a catch-22. We need change, but the planets are in a tug of war, forcing us to deal with a large segment of population that is acting out of fear and cannot accept transformation. Like Doc Daneeka suggested, we are crazy and destined to continue flying combat missions day after day.

So, what should we do?

The answer is given at the end of the year, auspiciously, right on the darkest day of the year, the Winter Solstice of 2020. On December 21, 2020, we experience something astrologers call the "Great Conjunction" of Jupiter (expansion) and Saturn (focus). The two planets both switch allegiance from conservative Capricorn to liberal Aquarius, the sign of humanism. The Grand Conjunction always signifies an end of one cycle and a beginning of another. The last time the two planets were conjunct was in May 2000, right as the dotcom bubble burst. Indeed, we can expect another bubble bursting in 2020. But, as any master builder or mason will tell you, demolition many times proceeds construction. I think that, instead of dreading death or change, we should become the change. From the beginning of 2020, we should use the diamond meditation to project into the collective unconscious how we would like this new era to manifest in our lives. Yes, we might be forced to step out of our comfort zone, but we should see it as an opportunity to find new places to build our abode. Change, it is a'coming. Let's fashion it in the image we would like.

22 Foundation Letters

"Twenty-Two Letters are the Foundation: He engraved them, He hewed them out, He combined them, and He set them at opposites, and He formed through them everything that is formed and everything that is destined to be formed."

Sefer Yetzirah (Book of Formation)

The *Book of Formation*, also known as the *Book of Creation*, is the oldest and arguably the most influential Kabbalistic text. Believed to have been written by the Biblical Patriarch Abraham, it is the first time the Tree of Life and its spheres are mentioned. It is a cryptic and enigmatic book that was used for centuries by seekers of the esoteric arts to create both inner and outer transformation.

The book is indeed a text of creation, explaining how God formed the universe and how we can follow his / her steps.

The book argues that God used the 22 Hebrew letters as the building blocks to create the universe. Each letter is associated with either a zodiac sign or a planetary archetype. It is no wonder that as early as the 18th and 19th century, mainly through the work of the occultist Eliphas Levi, the 22 Hebrew letters were assigned to the 22 Major Arcana cards of the tarot. I do follow these correlations in my private consultation and find them to be very accurate and helpful.

For example, the first Hebrew letter, *Alef*, in Kabbalah symbolizes air. The tarot card of the Fool is assigned the letter *Alef*, and as we already saw, "Fool" comes from the Latin, *follis*, windbag. The Fool card depicts a youth holding a bag of air, stepping off a cliff, making a leap of faith. The Fool is 0, but is also associated with 22, since there are 22 cards and the last one, the Universe, is assigned the number 21.

The Fool represents potential and, as mentioned before, contains the essence and seed of all the rest of the cards. We can see, once again, a convergence of myths, a theme that threads together different archetypes into a meaningful tapestry which we can use to cover ourselves against some of the stormy winds of 2020. Let's describe the story in terms of a Hollywood superhero blockbuster film where you are the star:

Act I

Ordinary World: A wave of populism and nationalism, fake politicians, fake news, disinformation, fearmongering, and warmongering.

The young are hopeless, suing governments around the world for stealing their future and bequeathing them a polluted world with rising sea levels and chaotic climate.

Inciting Incident: Jan 10 eclipse and Jan 12 Saturn and Pluto conjunction hit the earth. In addition, Mighty Mouse, the Metal Rat Year, kicks in Jan 25 and initiates a new cycle. Mighty Mouse, in his Metal (artificial intelligence) form, injects a special cosmic ray into you. The superhero / heroine within you awakens. You are confronted with a new reality, possibly in both your personal and professional life, that demands you make a leap of faith into a new field, sector, or environment. You hold the diamond on your mind's screen and, trusting in your new powers even though they are not fully developed, you take the leap. You experience your old life being demolished and feel alone. The old is melting away with no trace of the new in sight. You enter the dark forest of uncertainty.

Act II

In the end of March, an agent of change arrives into your life. Jupiter conjunct Pluto. This agent might appear in the form of a witch, a wizard, a mentor, teacher, guide, a great book, or anything that inspires you to begin developing your supernatural powers.

Pluto represents riches, power, magic, transformation, and Jupiter is enhancing his gifts. Remember, you are the Fool. No fear! In the bag of air, you have the 22 letters, the 22 Major Arcana.

You can be any card you like. You can be the Emperor (Aries) when you need to lead, or you can choose to be the High Priestess (Moon) when you need help from your subconscious or the spirit world. You are Death (Scorpio) if you need to demolish something you don't want in your life, and you are the Star (Aquarius) when you need to be seen and shine. In addition, at the end of March, Saturn abandons Capricorn and transits into Aquarius, the Star card. You absorb the extraterrestrial cosmic waves.

The middle of Act II is a low point. It feels like you are dying without physically dying. But, as Rumi once said, "Why should I fear death? When was I less by dying?" The June 5 eclipse is the first punch you receive from your antagonist, and the second comes on the Solstice, June 21, right on the solar eclipse. You feel like a solar flare hit you. But this is good, while you are laying there cataleptic and unconscious, it is the perfect time to gain access to the collective unconscious, the seat of all archetypes.

There, in a dreamlike state, while your enemies gloat thinking you are defeated, you will, in truth, accumulate all the tools you need to vanquish them. You will realize that the way you dealt with 2020 thus far did not work. Powering yourself through the hard aspects, fighting nonstop, overtraining, overworking, muscling through does not work.

A new tactic is needed, and this will be unveiled in July and August. Your Dragon appears in the shape of helpful people around August and in September. As Mars retrogrades, you return, a phoenix from the flame, ready to reclaim what is yours.

Act III

Remember, new tactic, new approach. Since Mars is retro, you do not want to start any conflicts. You are now the vessel of superheroes the like Gandhi, Jesus, Harriet Tubman, Eleanor Roosevelt, John Lennon, Nelson Mandela, Rosa Parks, Martin Luther King Jr., Henrietta Szold, Khan Abdul Ghaffar Khan, and millions of others who waged war on war in peaceful ways. Once Mars retrograde is over, in mid-November, right when Jupiter and Pluto meet again, you reconnect to the gift your wizard / witch gave you in the beginning of the year and you gain full access to your 22 letters of power. You are able to fully embody your superpowers and manifest your true potential.

You can now confront your antagonist (internal or external) one last time in the climax of the eclipses of December, but you also have help (Dec 14-25) from the "Great Conjunction," of Jupiter and Saturn in Aquarius, who send a comic cavalry to help you defeat the hordes of demons and trolls that surround you. You are finally crowned a Master Builder, gain your medal of recognition, and are ready to be the Jedi of Aquarius in 2021.

Big Bang Alignment – Pluto Conjunct Saturn

"I must not fear. Fear is the mind-killer. Fear is the little-death that brings total obliteration. I will face my fear. I will permit it to pass over me and through me. And when it has gone past, I will turn the inner eye to see its path. Where the fear has gone there will be nothing. Only I will remain."

Frank Herbert, Litany Against Fear Incantation of the Bene Gesserit, Dune

For many years now, Astrologers of different persuasions have been warning, anticipating, dreading, and prophesizing great disasters for the end of 2019 and the beginning of 2020. The reason is the triple conjunction of Pluto, the archetype of raw power and passion, with Saturn, the epitome of harsh lessons, the devourer of souls. I think you get the picture.

In addition, Jupiter, who usually comes to the rescue, moved into Capricorn in December 2019 to join the fray. Jupiter does not like to be in Capricorn, his sign of fall. Jupiter represents opportunities, luck, and flow, but while transiting in rigid Capricorn, he feels blocked and restricted. So, the rescue is somewhat diminished. To make things worse, Jupiter's tendency to expand might swell the destructive qualities of Saturn's union with Pluto. Since this drama takes place on the Capricorn stage, there is a very high probability for a recession or at least a major slowdown in the world economy. We will have to channel the frugal qualities of Capricorn in 2020 and be extra aware of needless expenses. The conjunction of Saturn (the furthest planet visible by the naked eye) and Pluto (the utmost "planet" from the Sun) acts like a New Moon. It represents a new beginning, a turning point, a flipping of a page in the story of humanity, an opening of a new file.

The conjunction is going back to square 1, opening opportunities while closing others. The year 2020, with all its conjunctions (Pluto / Saturn, Pluto / Jupiter, Jupiter / Saturn) is truly a new journey of the fool.

It is said that a pattern can only be identified using three occurrences. Here is a little sample of the last three times Saturn and Pluto joined forces. I recommend that you look back on these years to try to identify how these cycles manifested in your personal or familial history.

1982 / 1983: The rise of conservatives in the US (Ronald Reagan) and in the UK (Margaret Thatcher) and the escalation of the Cold War.

The US suffers a severe recession with the unemployment rate at 12 million, the worst since the Great Depression. Ethiopia suffers the worst drought in history and over 4 million die of hunger. In 1982, the CDC identifies a new epidemic as AIDS and in 1983 World Health Organization (WHO) holds its first meeting to discuss the global AIDS situation. [Side note, this could mean that in 2020 there will be major breakthrough with AIDS medication or eradication.] *Time Magazine* choses "The Computer" as the person of the year and Microsoft Word, which is what I am using to write this book, is launched. Motorola introduces the first mobile phones. Themes: technological and communication breakthrough, slowdown in economy, epidemics.

1946 / 1947: WWII comes to an end with a new world order led by the US. The US initiates the Marshall Plan to help rebuild Europe, infusing the devastated continent with 12 billion dollars. The Cold War begins. India, Pakistan, Israel, and North Korea, all nuclear nations today, gain independence. [Side note: these countries are close to half of the nations with nuclear weapon capabilities today. Pluto = Plutonium.] The U.N. creates WHO, the World Health Organization and adopts the Universal Declaration of Human Rights. Increased cases of polio around the world. Sound barrier is broken, humans travel faster than the speed of sound and the first mobile phone is invented. Themes: Rebuilding, technological advances, epidemics, change in financial structures.

1914 / 1915: World War I begins and the old power structures and empires collapse (Ottoman, British, Austro-Hungarian, Russian). First use of poisonous gas in warfare, first mass death from a war (37 million). The suffrage movement is in full swing with 25,000 women marching up 5th Ave in NY, demanding the right to vote. The first transcontinental telephone call as well as the first US coast-to-coast long-distance telephone call by Bell. Themes: war, new ways to kill people, liberation through pain, technological advances.

As you can see from the short time travel there is an emphasis on communication (phone and mobile), this might be a hint about the looming battle over 5G and communication technologies and / or a breakthrough with new forms of telecommunication.

2020 promises to be very intense, to put it mildly. We can dig deeper and locate historical incidents when Saturn and Pluto conjunct specifically in Capricorn:

783 CE the rise of Charlemagne, while the Vikings begin their expeditions towards Russia and later, Europe.

1284 CE Kublai Khan emperor of China. Marco Polo travels the silk road and, according to Lüneburg manuscript, a piper in Hamelin leads 130 children away.

1518 CE conquest of Mexico and the fall of the Aztec empire. This is also the year of the strange Dancing Plague, which begins with a woman in Strasbourg who started dancing and shaking for a week and close to 40 other people join the nonstop twirl. Within a month, 400 people die from dancing. In Wittenberg, Germany, Martin Luther begins his reformation.

We can infer from these precedents that old structures, financial or political, tend to collapse and change rapidly, giving space for something new. There is also a disturbing theme of original new ways of dying (Pluto), whether from unidentified viruses, poisonous gas, trench warfare, crazed dancing, or climate (drought). Knowing these pitfalls, it is our duty in our personal lives, as well as socially, to fight our tendency to fear for ourselves while neglecting others. Saturn is the Lord of Karma, as in action and reaction. Therefore, our actions and reactions (Saturn) to whatever Pluto (death and transformation) brings, can determine the outcome on a personal as well as global level.

Spellbound:
The Jupiter-Pluto Conjunction

The year 2020 sparkles with powerful conjunctions, but
the most magical one is the Jupiter-Pluto alignment.
Pluto is the ruler of Scorpio and the Lord of the
Underworld. He is the ruler of raw intensity,
uncontrolled urges, occult, transformation, the Freudian
id, healing and killing, a true wildling, or maybe even a
White-Walker. When Pluto moved into Capricorn, in
2008, the Great Recession began, and the last time he was
in Capricorn, the US was born.

When Pluto is in Capricorn, the goat sign, he transforms
into the Greek god Pan, who has the hindquarters, legs,
and horns of a goat, while the rest is very human. He is
the god of wilderness, mountains, sexual desire (even
though he is barren), and tends to be associated with
uncontrolled urges and passion; hence the many stories
from myth where he rapes both women and men.

He is associated with fear and the word "panic" is
derived from his name. But, with the influence of Jupiter,
the king of the gods, in conjunction with Pluto, Pan
transforms into Peter Pan. He still has the pan flute and
the green outfit of the forest. He is charming and
flirtatious, somewhat unpredictable, but far kinder and
more loveable.

The last time these two planets were conjunct, Al Gore received his Nobel Prize for work on climate change. We can expect more discoveries about renewable energies, changes in how we work with energy and power as well as a surge of positive healing and new medications. In 2020, we have three conjunctions of Pluto and Jupiter: we will meet Peter Pan thrice — April 5, June 30, and November 13. However, the influence will be felt a week before and a few days after these dates. Since Pluto also rules other people's talents and money, as well as inheritance and investments, 2020 is a good year to collaborate, initiate joint artistic or financial projects, and explore hidden talents in you as well as in your partners. Remember, Pluto is often associated with the occult, wizards and witches, warlocks and healers. Jupiter enhances these qualities in you and in others.

The Dawning of the Age of Aquarius: Jupiter-Saturn Conjunction

"Imagine there's no countries. It isn't hard to do.
Nothing to kill or die for, and no religion, too."

John Lennon, Imagine

In astrology, there are four sacred days and they are the four cardinal points of the year: Spring Equinox (20 March), Summer Solstice (21 June), Vernal Equinox (22 Sep), and Winter Solstice (Dec 22). The dates change a bit every year and are reversed for the Southern Hemisphere. These days represent the four types of relationships between night and day, feminine and masculine, and their harmonious balance. The Equinoxes celebrate the perfect harmony between day and night (*equi*=equal; *nox*=night). The Solstice captures a moment in the year when either yin or yang energies are more pronounced, hence the longest night (Winter Solstice) or longest day (Summer Solstice).

The Equinoxes and Solstices are also the first day of each of the four seasons and therefore the reason why life evolved on earth.

If there were only winter or only summer, if we were only feminine or only masculine, there would be no life on the blue planet.

For this reason, any planet or alignment that falls on these four points is dramatically magnified in significance. In 2020, true to its intensity, we have a solar eclipse falling right on the Summer Solstice, as well as the "Great Conjunction" of Jupiter and Saturn taking place precisely on the Winter Solstice. These are two powerful synchronicities, since both are conjunctions, representing an end of a cycle and a beginning of a new one. Ouroboros: the serpent that bites its own tail. A powerful message at the middle and the end of the year: 2020 is a turning point.

Saturn and Jupiter are conjunct every 20 years and in the last 220 years their conjunction has always taken place in earth signs (except for 1980 / 1981, when it was in Libra). For 220 years, we dealt with earth-related issues. For instance, the Industrial Revolution used coal as an energy source, which was later replaced with fossil fuel and uranium, all coming from the earth. In the last few years, we even started using rare earth elements in our electronic devices. But in 2020, the conjunction of Jupiter and Saturn is moving into air signs. The air signs are open, accepting, and far less traditional.

The air signs, Libra, Aquarius, and Gemini, emphasize and represent communication, relationship, interconnectedness, trade, globalization, invention, technology, and space exploration.

Together with the Metal Rat year, I think we can safely say we are officially entering the Age of Aquarius, the age of artificial intelligence.

The Saturn-Jupiter conjunction in Aquarius is a return to the qualities that this sign represents: freedom, equality, emancipation, democracy, innovation, technology, sharing economy, awareness, and the recognition that all humans are created equal. Since Pluto is still in Capricorn until 2023 / 2024, we will experience a pull and push between forces that want to build walls (Capricorn) and forces that want to build windmills and other renewable energies (Aquarius).

On a personal level, you might feel the urge to join groups, to volunteer, to take on a humanitarian cause, to add or change some of your friends. Since the conjunction takes place on the Winter Solstice, the longest night (Northern Hemisphere), there will be a change in government in many places above the equator. Maybe a global winter blues that can affect the economy and consumer trust, but there could also be a scientific breakthrough in medicine and technology. In the Southern Hemisphere, the conjunction takes place on the longest day; therefore, there is a new dawn and hope coming from South America, Africa, and Australia.

Saturn in Aquarius

Saturn is the planet of karma and has been traditionally associated with limitations, restrictions, and difficulties. While that is true, we now look at Saturn as the great teacher, the one planet that exposes the truth and forces us to work hard for rewards. Saturn is the strict yoga teacher forcing the chair pose to be held lower and longer, the personal trainer who does not let you give up, and the challenging book that makes you read each paragraph three times. In the Kabbalistic Tree of Life, Saturn is associated with the sphere *Understanding* (Binah), the archetype of the Great Mother.

Since the end of 2017, Saturn has been in Capricorn and we have seen the global level of fear rise like a tide. The talk of us versus them, trade wars, enriching uranium, building walls, locking children up, and the mass spread of misinformation took over current events. However, Saturn is always on the move and every 2 ½ years, he changes his focus. From March 22 until July 2, 2020, and then again from December 17, 2020 until March 6, 2023, Saturn is hosted by Aquarius.

The last time Saturn was in Aquarius was Feb 1991 – Feb 1994 and Jan 1962 – March 1964. It is important to go back to those dates, since the root of your "Understanding" of 2020 – 2023 can be traced back to them. If you were born then, well, welcome to Saturn Return, which I write about extensively in my book on astrology, *Cosmic Navigator.*

Saturn in Aquarius is like a contractor hired to do a major makeover of your house of friends and community. Some people will change their political affiliation, join new groups, let go of companies, change their workplace, discover affinities to nonprofit or humanitarian groups, and focus on government and corporations. Globally, there will be a great deal of reshuffling in political systems around the world. In Europe and the US, however, there is a darker side to Saturn in Aquarius. We must all take heed as Saturn was also in Aquarius during the rise of fascism, 1933 – 1935. But the good news is that, in the 30s, we did not have Jupiter in Aquarius, which creates an abundance of peaceful enhancement of the Aquarius qualities of altruism and friendliness, at least at the end of 2020 and throughout 2021.

In April, May, and June, 2020, when Saturn exits Capricorn, you feel a change in the wind, a lighter energy. At the same time, patterns and insecurities (Saturn) with your friends and / or organization (Aquarius) can surface. These three months are a precursor of what is to come in 2021 and 2022.

I suggest you clean the slate of your friendships before March and evaluate how authentic you feel with your friends, groups, clubs, companies, and organizations. In personal relationships, try to focus more on deepening your friendships, and try to befriend your partner's friend or make new common friends. Since Aquarius is also associated with technology, give your life a technological facelift. In Part II, I will explain how Saturn moving into Aquarius manifests in your sign.

Jupiter in Capricorn

From December 3, 2019 until December 19, 2020, Jupiter, the planet representing unlimited opportunities, is transiting in Capricorn. If you are a Capricorn, Taurus, or Virgo, you will benefit from this transit. Aries, Libra, and Cancer might feel a bit awkward with Jupiter, causing them to take actions they might regret or not feel comfortable with. Capricorns will welcome this transit as it is a burden to have Pluto, the South Node, as well as Saturn in their sign. However, Jupiter does not feel good in Capricorn. Jupiter likes to spend, he is generous and optimistic, but Capricorn symbolizes scrutiny and audit, tight budgets, and restrictions. Therefore, the usual expansive qualities of Jupiter are constricted. This is another reason we expect an economic slowdown in 2020.

Please check the dates below to see what transpired in your life in previous periods where Jupiter was transiting through Capricorn. The gifts synchronized with Jupiter in Capricorn are a bit subtle but can still be identified since it happens every 12 years.

Look back at the dates below and try to identify patterns of benevolence and opportunity. Which doors opened?

What happened then that you would like to repeat in 2020? Sometimes having a goal helps Jupiter bestow his gifts.

Aug 13, 1961 – Nov 3, 1961; Feb 7, 1972 – Feb 23, 1973; Jan 19, 1984 – Feb 6, 1985; Jan 3, 1996 – Jan 21, 1997; Dec 19, 2007 – Jan 5, 2009.

The North Node Transition

The Moon's North and South Nodes, also called the "Head" and "Tail of the Dragon," or the "Nodes of Fate," travel backward in the zodiac wheel and change signs about every 18 months. The North and South Nodes always occupy opposite signs and represent opposite forces. While the North Node, the Head of the Dragon, points at the sign whose lessons we are required to learn and embody, the South Node, or the Tail of the Dragon, points at the sign we must unlearn and let go of in order to grow. From November 2018 until June 2020, the North Node is in Cancer and, therefore, the South Node is in Capricorn. From June 5, 2020, until December 22, 2021, the North Node is in Gemini and the South in Sagittarius. The last time the Nodes were in Gemini / Sagittarius was October 2001 to May 2003. The Nodes are the intersection, and therefore, the crossroads, between the paths of the Moon and the Sun.

And for this reason, whatever sign the Nodes occupy is also the sign of the eclipses. When the North Node is in Gemini, it asks us to assume the positive and spiritual aspects of Gemini, which include sharing information, improving communication, treating every person we meet as if he or she was our sibling, learning to be objective and not take things so personally. There is a lightness in Gemini (an air sign) that we so desperately need in such a heavy Capricorn (earth sign) year. Since the South Node is in Sagittarius, we all need to let go of the darker aspects of Sagittarius which include fanaticism, radicalism (left or right), zealotry, gluttony, over-optimism, and thinking our truth is the Truth. Gemini is a mutable (changing and unpredictable) air sign. When we have the North Node in Gemini, we must connect to air, which means *breathing* — we are wise to practice breathing exercises in the next 18 months. You can try the 4-2-4-2 technique: breathe in for the count of four; hold the breath in for the count of two; breathe out for the count of 4; and hold the air out for the count of 2. Doing this exercise for 10 minutes a day will help you ride the Dragon like a pro. Also recommended are any cardio activities that you enjoy: running, kickboxing, swimming, hiking, cycling, dancing—anything that can force your lungs (Gemini's body part) to work hard. If you smoke, well, quit!

Right when the North Node moves into Gemini, Venus will be retrograde in the same sign (May 13 until June 25).

This retro is another interesting synchronicity that forces us to focus on relationships in a year where numbers are double 2s. Venus retrograde helps us reevaluate our partners in work and in life. Venus can change our "love map," our love schemas we hold in our heads and hearts that contains what we are attracted to as well as who we attract. Since the North Node and Venus are both in Gemini, we are encouraged to find love (Venus) with our relatives (Gemini) as well as develop or add brotherly / sisterly (Gemini) feelings in our partners (Venus) in love or business.

Since Mercury is the ruler of Gemini, the retrogrades in the next two years are going to be extra significant and powerful. They will become landmarks for identifying and undoing karma from past lives. In the chapters of the zodiac signs, I will explain what Mercury and Venus retro mean specifically to the different astrological signs.

Eclipses in 2020

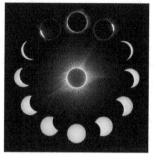

Eclipses quicken processes and push events towards completion. Susan Miller articulately calls them "wild cards." They amplify whatever is happening in your life, forcing a resolution through confrontation. Eclipses are storytellers that use synchronicities, omens, and dreams as magical life-changing stanzas. I like to think of eclipses as if they are the city plaza of the year, a beautiful crossroads adorned with a fountain, a monument, and a bazar. The eclipses bring about change even if at first you cannot identify it, like in chaos theory, when something that seems insignificant (flapping of a butterfly wing) can create a storm. There are two types of eclipses:

SOLAR ECLIPSES are powerful New Moons when the Sun and the Moon are conjunct at the same place. The Moon's disk covers the Sun and we feel neglected, alone, hopeless, and experience a lack of vitality. Since the Sun disappears, we feel as if daddy left us alone. In the Solar eclipse, you might feel lightless, devastated, or blocked, but it is usually because the path you were on was leading nowhere.

However, Solar eclipses, true to their New Moon qualities, present a new beginning, a new road that opens usually right when another closes. Usually Solar eclipses are concerned with action, over-rationalization, movement, and making decisions.

LUNAR ECLIPSES are augmented Full Moons. We on Earth are caught right between the Moon and the Sun. We are pushed and pulled between mom and dad, like a divorce child in a custody battle. The Lunar eclipses tend to be emotional, psychosomatic, draining, and eventful. While the Solar eclipse is masculine, the Lunar eclipse is the wild aspect of femininity. It is associated with werewolves, creatures of the night, magic, transformation, subconscious fears, the astral plane, instincts, and fear. During the Lunar eclipse, fight the urge to be reactive. Just breathe deeply and let things go. It is a good time to practice surrender and cut away things that block you.

In 2020, we have the greatest number of eclipses possible in one year. We are maxed out. Below is the list of eclipses, as well as their paths, which show where they manifest most strongly. The most powerful eclipse takes place on the Solstice June 21. In addition, a Lunar eclipse takes place right on US Independence Day. When an eclipse happens five days before or after a birthday (of a person, company, or nation), it can point to a health issue or a drastic transformation taking place. Since it is happening to the US right on the onset of the nation's Saturn and Pluto return, it signifies a major change of direction. Any attempts to hold on to the past will face grave consequences.

There are three types of eclipses: total (35% of all eclipses), partial (30%), and penumbral (35%). As you can see from the list below, four of the eclipses are penumbral. In this type, only the outer shadow of the Earth falls on the Moon's surface, making it the most subtle, and hardest to observe of all the eclipses.

I have also added the Sabian oracle symbols for each eclipse, which give an image or a short metaphor that captures the essence of the lunation. As many astrologers before me, I find these symbols rather peculiar, but often also helpful and eerily accurate.

Jan 10 / 11: Penumbral Lunar eclipse in Cancer. Sabian symbol: Prima donna singing. Eclipse path: Europe, Asia, Australia, Africa, much of North America, east in South America, Pacific, Atlantic, Indian Ocean. This eclipse is a push and pull between career and home. The need to help others and the fear of not having enough. This Lunar eclipse takes place while Saturn, Mercury, and Pluto are opposite to the Moon, which adds to the tension. This eclipse can be challenging emotionally with a great deal of manipulation, especially since it is two days before the dreaded conjunction of Pluto and Saturn. Take heed. Remember, the North Node is in Cancer, which gives priority to home, family, security, and compassion.

June 5 / 6: Penumbral Lunar eclipse in Sagittarius. Sabian symbol: Seagulls watching a ship. Eclipse path: much of Europe, much of Asia, Australia, Africa, south / east South America, Pacific, Atlantic, Indian Ocean.

This eclipse is the first of the new Gemini-Sagittarius eclipses. Truth versus lies; authentic against fake. Revelation of hidden information and data. This eclipse takes place while Venus is retrograde and conjunct the Sun adding relationships issues to the mix. In addition, Mars is squaring the eclipse and Venus. This planetary mix emphasis the square aspect of 2020 we discussed earlier when we mentioned the number 4 and its qualities. Diplomatic incidents, relationship quarrels, insecurities surface that can hinder partnerships and present challenges with finance.

June 21: Solar Annular Solstice eclipse in Cancer.
Sabian symbol: A sailor ready to hoist a new flag to replace an old one. Eclipse path: south / east Europe, much of Asia, north Australia, much of Africa, Pacific and Indian Oceans. In an annual eclipse (from the word *annulus* – ring), the Moon passes right over the center of the Sun but leaves the edges of the Solar disk uncovered, hence the appearance of a ring. "One ring to rule them all and in the darkness bind them," as J. R. R. Tolkien suggested. This eclipse falls right on the Solstice and therefore is far more powerful. The Sun and the Moon are close to the North Node in Gemini, forcing us to look deep into our message for this lifetime. The eclipse will bind together communication and emotions, thoughts and feelings, words and sensations. This eclipse opens a new pathway for humanity, since the Summer Solstice is often called the "Gateway of Humanity."

In addition, this eclipse takes place during a retrograde bonanza: Mercury, Venus, Pluto, Saturn, Pallas, and

Jupiter are all in retrograde motion. This means their expression is more internal and awkward. Take extra care of how you talk, relate, and communicate with lovers, friends, and authority figures.

July 4 / 5: Penumbral Lunar eclipse in Capricorn. Sabian symbol: An ancient bas-relief carved in granite. Eclipse path: south / west Europe, much of Africa and North America, South America, Pacific, Atlantic, Indian Oceans. This eclipse is the mirror image of the Lunar eclipse of January 10, and therefore continues whatever we started then. Uranus is sending a trine to the eclipse Moon, adding a spark of positive unexpected news. Since the eclipse falls right on the US birthday, a big change is happening in the world's biggest economy and the leader of the free world. It is a Full Moon, which often describes an ending and a change of course. Mercury is retrograde during this eclipse; therefore, you can expect to continue having miscommunication. Take heed with actions, choices, words, and what you put out there.

Nov 29 / 30: Penumbral Lunar eclipse in Gemini. Sabian symbol: Quiver filled with arrows. Eclipse path: much of Europe and Asia, Australia, North America, South America, Pacific, Atlantic. The eclipse continues the exploration of what is true and what is false. It is a time to change the way we learn and teach, and we may see changes in mass media and communication outlets. Watch your relationships with relatives and in-laws.

Dec 14: Total Solar eclipse in Sagittarius. Sabian symbol: Blue bird standing at the door of the house. Eclipse path: South Africa, much of South America, Pacific, Atlantic, Indian Oceans. A powerful eclipse that begins a new journey in education, travel, and publishing. You might encounter an inspiring mentor or become one for someone else. Pay attention to a specific culture, country, or foreigner who might inspire you to start something new in your life. This eclipse is a great time to start learning a new language.

The Year of the White Metal Rat

From January 21, 2020 until February 11, 2021, the world will be swarmed by little metal robotic rats. It sounds terrible to Westerners who, in their genes, in their ancestral memories, as well as in past life memories, remember the last time rats came from the East bearing fleas that spread the Black Death of the 14th century. But in China, the Year of the Rat is a source of celebration. We also have some good rats to offset the negative connotations. Think of Mighty Mouse who comes to save the day, or Mickey Mouse, or the Rat Pack, etc. 2020 will be a great year to release the Mighty Mouse movie if any of you reading these words are involved in the adaptation.

One day, the Buddha, being a Taurus and a true son of Mother Earth, decided to invite the animals to meditate with him. You know, Noah, who was probably a water sign, invited the animals on a cruise, and the Buddha, modest as ever, just wanted to share space with the animals of the forest. He knew there are 12 months to the year and that Jupiter takes 12 years to orbit the Sun, and so he proclaimed that the first 12 animals that came to him would be chosen to be part of the "animal wheel," and that the order of their arrival would determine the sequence of their signs.

The news was faithfully spread by the wind, and soon many animals started their journey to the Buddha, wanting to make sure they were not only included but were also vying for the lead. The horse begun galloping. The dragon spread his wings. The pig, the cat, and the cockroach all started to race towards the Buddha. However, the Buddha was sitting under a Bodhi tree across a wide river. The ox was happy since the river was his home. He only needed to cross and make his appearance. Just when he made his first step, he saw a rat and a tiny Bengal tiger that looked like a cat. At that time, they were inseparable best friends. The cute rat and cat charmed the ox with small talk and compliments and asked if he could give them a lift across the water since they both did not swim. The ox, feeling generous, agreed to help them cross and the friends hopped on his back. Right before they reached the other bank, the rat showed his true colors and pushed the cat off the ox, jumping over the ox's head to the other bank, and stood in front of the Buddha.

That is why the rat is the first in the zodiac, the ox the second, and the wet cat (tiger) third. That is also why cats to this day run after rats. The Buddha was not fooled, and he could have easily disqualified the cheater, and maybe he should have. But I think, if I may justify the inaction of the Buddha, that he wanted to send a message to all the small, unable, disenfranchised, and poor, that they always have a chance to be the leader.

Then again, who knows what really happened on the back of the ox. Maybe the cat wanted to push the rat but he managed somehow to perform a tai chi move that sent the cat off. Maybe the ox got something from the rat? I guess the tale of the rat winning the race is the Chinese version of the David and Goliath story. The white rat in Japan and China, which is associated with the Year of the Metal Rat, is a sign of luck and good fortune. In Japan, rats were the companion of the god of luck, Daikokuten, who is also the lord of five cereals. It makes mythological sense, as rats are found where there is rice, wheat, and food. In ancient Greece and Rome, white rats were also a sign of good fortune and were associated with Apollo, who was the god of light, music, dance, and healing, but also of plague. In India, Lord Ganesha, the remover of obstacles, is often depicted riding a big mouse or rat. In the past, rodents were a great obstacle, eating grain, destroying crops, and spreading diseases. It is appropriate for the remover of obstacles to conquer and tame, therefore ride on the back of a rat.

The Year of the Metal Rat is starting a new 12-year cycle, true to the astrological nature of 2020 with its many conjunctions. The rat, in Chinese astrology, is highly respected and many parents long to have a baby born under this sign. The rat is wise, cunning, inventive, crafty, original, ambitious, and driven. Add the metal element, and you are getting a robot-rat.

No wonder next year will be a year where the 5G battle lines will be drawn on the global map. However, the rat can also be ruthless (like pushing his best friend into the river to get ahead), a true believer in "the end justifies the means," he is prone to nervousness and anxiety. This is another indication that 2020 is a panic attack sort of year, along with what we already discussed earlier with the Pluto-Saturn-Pan conjunction.

Previous Year of the Rat: 1936, 1948, 1960, 1972, 1984, 1996, 2008. Also, 1960 and 1900 were the other years of the Metal Rat.

Judging from the astrological transitions coming up in the next 12 years, with Uranus (technology) moving into Gemini (binary) and Pluto (power) into Aquarius (futuristic), the new Chinese astrology cycle initiated by the metal element could mean we can expect artificial intelligence to finally be integrated in our lives and get the leap we were expecting for decades.

New Year's Resolution

Timing is everything and astrology can help with your 2020 New Year's Resolution. To have a successful resolution manifest, you have to make sure you don't only formulate the right wish but also start the process of actualization at the right time. Below are a few dates that are auspicious to begin making your 2020 dream come true. Make sure you choose a resolution that is focused on you. Don't select a resolution that someone else wants for you. Try to ensure that the wish has an emotional component and that you can add a number to it. For example, I want to make more money. Well, how much? I want to get a new apartment. How big? I want to lose weight. How many kilos? Between February 16 – March 10, Mercury is retrograde and it is not a good time for a new beginning. My very good friend and bestselling author, Laura Day, wrote a book that can truly help with making your New Year's resolution a success: The Circle: How the power of a single wish can change your life (Atria Books 2001).

Jan 6 – If your resolution is for a long-term goal and you need a great deal of discipline to achieve it.

Jan 10 – Eclipse and grand conjunction. Chose this date only if your wish has to do with letting go and cutting something out of your life: quitting a substance or an addiction, leaving a toxic relationship.

Jan 25 – New Moon in Aquarius, the sign of making wishes come true. It is also the Chinese New Year.

Jan 28 – Conjunction of Moon, Venus, and Neptune. Good for wishes that relate to relationships, art, creativity, yoga, dance, and meditation.

Feb 23 – New Moon in Pisces. ONLY if you want to undo something in your life or reconnect to an old project you neglected since Mercury is retrograde.

March 20 – Spring Equinox: The Astrological New Year.

Uranus, the Fool

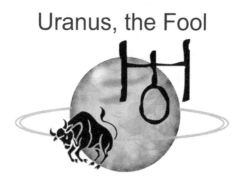

Uranus is the great awakener, but sometimes he feels more like chaos and disorder. He represents unpredictable and revolutionary behavior. In history, he has been the bearer of change and is associated with innovation and sparks of genius. Uranus spends about seven years in each sign, sort of a planetary seven-year itch. Uranus first moved into Taurus in May 2018, and has been there consistently since March 2019. Taurus is the sign of finance, promising to create a revolution in the world's economy, maybe giving a push to alternative financial systems.

Since Taurus is also the sign of values, finance, art, design, and music, Uranus transit in the sign until 2026 provides an opportunity to shift and change these aspects in our lives. When the market is doing well, we call it the Bull Market as the bull or cow has always represented wealth, prosperity, and security. In the ancient world, the number of cows a family possessed was an indicator of their wealth. Think about the term "cash cow," something that you can always milk for more profits. Uranus in Taurus is here to shake the financial tree, but Taurus is a fixed earth sign.

It is a sign that does not like to move or change. That is why we can expect a great deal of upheaval in the next few years as Uranus settles in this stubborn, fixed, earth sign.

Uranus in Taurus can also instigate big discoveries and breakthroughs in science, medicine (hair growth, Alzheimer's, Cancer, AIDS), and computing, as well as the rise of an artificial intelligence-based economy. Of course, these trends can cause a great deal of upsets, revolutions, and protests from people who might lose their livelihood to machines. This process will continue even after April 2026, when Uranus moves to Gemini, the binary sign. During that decade (2026-2037), we can expect machines to process information faster than humans. Uranus' transit in Taurus can also manifest as society in general and each one of us personally, questioning and reevaluating our values, beliefs, and creeds.

Right when Uranus moved into Taurus, the EU declared its GDPR (General Data Protection Regulations) which changed the way data can be mined and used by technology companies. California is said to follow soon. The cycle of Uranus is 84 years. The last time Uranus was in Taurus was during the Great Depression and the onset of World War II. In the US, during Uranus in Taurus, the Social Security Act (1935) as well as the Banking Act (which changed the structure and power distribution of the Federal Reserve system) became the law of the land. For the last nine decades, the US dollar has been the most dominant currency, but Uranus in the sign of finance and money will most likely change its status. On a personal level, when Uranus is in Taurus, we are asked to rethink our finances and investigate upgrading and innovating our talents. It is a time to expect some changes in our income and maybe take a leap of faith into a new field or a new source of revenue. We should avoid any radical investments and be extra careful with cryptocurrency. Remember, Uranus is technology and Taurus is finance. We can expect more cyber (Uranus) attacks, especially on banks and financial institutions (Taurus). However, there could be more natural disasters and climate change as Taurus is said to be associated with Mother Nature.

At the end of the year and throughout 2021, Uranus will be squaring Saturn. This can indicate revolutions and financial upsets, especially among people who will not accept the Aquarian change promised by the Jupiter Saturn conjunction in December.

This Uranus-Saturn square pits the forces of the status quo and conservativism with those of liberalism and freedom. It might manifest as a powerful struggle between the millennials and the more conservatives among the Baby Boomers.

Uranus in Taurus can give us the opportunity to revolutionize our artistic expression, our economy, and the way we treat our environment. While it is true that Uranus can be disruptive, his nature is to awaken us from behaviors or attitudes that sedate us into feeling comfortably numb or help us change things that don't work to our advantage or which keep us asleep. Uranus asks us to laugh at ourselves.

Tarot Cards of 2020

Below is a list of the most significant tarot cards of the
year. You can also go online and google the cards, print
out your favorite versions, and use them in your
meditations:

THE FOOL – The most important Major Arcana card of
this year, mainly because of its numerological
significance and its relevance for 2020. The card's
number is 0 and symbolizes a new journey and the leap
of faith from potential to actual.

THE HIGH PRIESTESS – The Major Arcana card of the
Moon. Since this year we have six eclipses, the Moon is
very dominant. An interesting synchronicity is that the
number of the card is 2.

2 OF DISKS – The card is called "Change," and its
astrological correlation is Jupiter in Capricorn. This card
symbolizes a positive change in career and vocation — a
slow, methodical, planned transition into a better
position in your professional life.

2 OF WANDS – The card is dubbed "Dominion,"
astrologically it is associated with Mars in Aries. This
year Mars will spend the last six months in Aries. This
card represents the need to push forward, take control
over your life, and avoid being passive.

As you surely noticed, the cards of the major astrological
transits of the year 2020 happen to all be 2s and 0s.

Age of Aquarius?

*"And these children that you spit on, as they
try to change their worlds, are immune to your
consultations. They're quite aware of what
they're going through. Ch-ch-ch changes…"*
David Bowie, Changes, Hunky Dory

Where are we headed? What is the state of the world?
When does the Age of Aquarius finally arrive? These are
questions I am asked all over the world by individuals,
companies, and media outlets. Russian President,
Vladimir Putin, made headlines in the 2019 G20 Summit,
saying in an interview to the Financial Times that
liberalism is obsolete. He further claimed that liberal
ideas about refugees, migration, and LGBT issues were
now opposed by "the overwhelming majority of the
population."

Of course, Putin has no clue of what the majority of the population thinks, and it is common knowledge that everything coming out of his mouth is part of an everlasting disinformation propaganda campaign, but he voices ideas that many other strongmen hold.

In the last decade we have seen the rise of reactionary far-right, nationalism, and populism. I believe this is a pushback against the forces of the Age of Aquarius, the era we are now entering, an epoch that is colored by tolerance, globalization, fraternity of humankind, interconnectedness, democratic ideals, and equality. I feel that since globalization is so engraved in our lives that mostly uneducated people who feel left out are trying to reverse the clock back to a fantastical imaginary time in the past when life was simple. The "good old days," with clear labels and definitions. A time when men looked and behaved like men and could only marry women. A world where Europeans were white Christians, Jews confined in ghettos, women in the kitchen, and blacks in the cotton fields. A glorious time when America was great and only men played soccer. However, millennials and Generation Z around the world remind us in their utter and absolute acceptance of diversity that the train of globalization left the station and there is no turning back. Aquarius – the Age of Oneness is here to stay.

In the last decade, since the beginning of the Great Recession, Pluto, representing power, has been transiting in Capricorn. Capricorn's dark side is fear of survival. That is why Capricorn's tarot card is called "the Devil."

The card represents our collective fear: that there is not enough for everyone. Capricorn is about building walls and barriers, fortifications, and fences.

However, in 2023-2024, right when Putin's term is supposed to end, Pluto will move into Aquarius for almost two decades. During these twenty years we should be feeling the full force of the Age of Aquarius. In 2020, as Saturn transits into Aquarius (March – early July, and again from December 2020 until 2022), we should feel a change as the crest of the Capricorn influence should start ebbing. Of course, Jupiter moving into Aquarius in December 2020 for a year should help show people the benefits of recognizing that there is "neither Jew nor Gentile, neither slave nor free, nor is there male and female, for you are all one" (Galatians 3:28).

Putin is wrong, and so are all the other self-serving racist old white men that seem to somehow be (mis)leading the world now. Liberalism is not dead; it is just dressed in green. In the summer of 2019, the German Green Party received 27% support becoming the biggest party in Germany. The party won 20% in the European elections and they were the most popular among all voters under the age of 60. In France the Greens became the most popular party among voters under 35.

Millennials as well as members of the Gen Z are taking their future into their own hands, demanding that ignorant and self-serving politicians recognize the looming ecological disasters they are creating. The youngsters filling up the Green Parties' ranks recognize that only global solutions can help fight climate change. You might clean your act in your city, state, or country, but if the neighboring nation continues using fossil fuel, the pollution will cross any wall you build. Smog, so it seems, does not need a visa to immigrate. To save humanity, to clean the world, to end hunger and war, to cure diseases, we need world unity, we need Aquarius, we need to let go of patriotism and reconnect to humanism. It is the future. LET IT HAPPEN NOW.

2020 Affirmation

I am ready to take a leap of faith and welcome, accept, and create a new life. I act out of trust and fearlessness, knowing that the more I give, the more I receive. 2020 is the year where my career, community, and talents merge into a happy, productive, and successful life.

Let's Go!

In some of the sections, I refer to the element of your sign. You will see that I would call a Leo, a fire sign, a Fire-Bender, or a Scorpio, a water sign, a Water-Bender. This is a homage to the wonderful animated Nickelodeon TV series, (2005) *Avatar: The Last Air Bender*. If you have a kid or an active inner child, watch this wonderful series that helps balance the elements in an entertaining way. Aries, Leo, and Sagittarius are Fire-Benders; Gemini, Libra, and Aquarius are Air-Benders; Cancer, Scorpio, and Pisces are Water-Benders;

Capricorn, Taurus, and Virgo are Earth-Benders.

In Part II, the following section, you will find sentences like: "Jupiter is in your house of career," or "Venus enters your house of health." In astrological charts, there are 12 houses that symbolize areas in our lives like career, health, relationships, etc.

You don't have to worry about what it all means, but I added the name of the houses for you to have more clarity and maybe spark an interest in studying this ancient art.

Since 2020 is associated with the 22 Hebrew letters, I added the letter assigned by Kabbalistic texts to each sign. You can use the image for your meditation or as a key to open hidden chambers of your subconscious. You can also choose to place the letter in the center of the diamond in your visualization meditation described below.

2020 is a year where we are all walking, like the Fool, on the cliff's edge. Yes, 2020 is a dangerous year, and true, it is a stormy time, but we have our inner guides and the powers of synchronicity on our side. 2020 is an adventurous year full of unexpected twists and turns. A year that favors the bold and courageous, those willing to take a chance but adhere to discipline, persistence, and perseverance.

Diamond Meditation

Sit in a comfortable position or lie flat on your back. Breathe deeply and relax yourself by using the 4-2-4-2 technique: breathing in for the count of four, holding the breath inside for the count of two, releasing the air for the count of four, and keeping it out for the count of two. Continue these cycles of breath and imagine you are conjuring a golden circle around you with your circular breath.

You are now in a center of a golden circle or sphere. Now imagine within the circle a silver square touching the circumference of the circle. You now focus your imagination to tilt the square 45 degrees so that the it transforms into a diamond with its four angles touching the circle. You are now seated within a diamond, surrounded with a ring. In each of the four corners, imagine four things you would like to materialize this year. In the diamond's corner located left of you, imagine something you would like to bring into your life that has to do with you personally, your body, your identity. In the right corner of the diamond, imagine something you want to manifest this year that has to do with relationships, partnership, and or collaborations. In the corner below you, imagine a wish that related to family, real estate, something that has an emotional component. Opposite, in the corner of the diamond located above your head, imagine something you want to bring into your life that relates to career and your professional life.

Now, that you are inside your diamond, within the circle, surrounded with the four items or images you wish to manifest this year, imagine the diamond rotating clockwise around its vertical axis. Imagine the rotation to be so fast that you can hardly see the diamond anymore. Take a few breaths while the diamond is swirling around you like a whirling dervish Sufi. After a few more breaths, slow the rotation. Imagine the diamond shrinks until it is small enough to fit, like a spiritual tattoo, on your forehead right at your third eye. The golden circle around you disappears and you come back to the here and now.

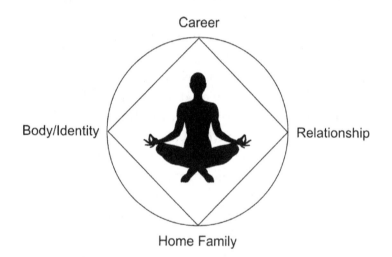

You can record the instruction of the meditation on your phone so you can play it whenever you need to use the meditation.

Part II

The Zodiac Signs in 2020

ARIES

New Karmic Cycle:
Career and Mission in Life

The year 2020 continues and deepens your focus on your career, community leadership, as well as your mission in life. Most of the conjunctions (new beginnings) take place in your house of career and professional life — being the Ram, these are super important to you. Since the end of 2017, you have been feeling the pressure to change, make adjustments, and prove yourself to your superiors or colleagues. In addition, in the last two years, you were asked to deal with a demanding boss or experience challenges or focus on father figures. This trend continues in 2020, however, since Saturn temporarily shifts into your house of community and friends (end of March until beginning of July). While experiencing some relief in your career, your focus and challenges turn to your company, friends, governments, and corporations. These few months will give you a glimpse of what lessons Saturn will teach you in 2021-2023. In addition, the end of March until the beginning of July will give you an opportunity to see who you can consider your true friends.

Make sure you pay taxes, apply for all the permits you need from the city or government, and play it cool with the authorities.

January of 2020 can be a bit rough, especially if you are born at the end of Aries (April 10 – 19). These challenges would mainly be felt in your career or with your bosses. If you are self-employed, it could manifest as hardships with employees or just being a bad boss to yourself. The powerful conjunction of Saturn / Pluto / Jupiter can manifest as a dramatic call to action, a need to change direction in life, or perhaps as a call to embark on a new adventure or a new conquest.

The good news is that you also have Jupiter, the planet of opportunities, transiting in your house of career. This is a new aspect; you did not have it in 2019. So you can accept new horizons opening in your professional life and recognition of your hard work. Maybe a raise or a promotion or a brilliant idea that can improve your career over time.

This is especially significant, since Uranus, the awakener, is in your house of finance and talent, creating chaos but also new possibilities around innovation, technology, and e-commerce. It is time to think outside of the box and welcome the future to the now. Uranus in the house of finance can be scary, since it is unpredictable and somewhat disruptive, but it can also, like the Fool, help you take a leap of faith into a new sector, profession, or position. Be open. Connect to your pioneering spirit! This year from June 28 to the end of the year, Mars, your planet will be in your sign!

That is huge, since Mars usually spends about six weeks in each sign. You will feel invincible, which is not always good during Mars retrograde (Sep 9 to Nov 14) as you might overextend yourself and start too many projects or engage in too many adventures. Pace yourself! You are running a marathon not a sprint. Mars in your house of leadership will feel like a call for action. It is time to take control and move forward. You are the ram, the leader of the zodiac, and you are being called this year to take charge and help us arrive at the uncharted territories of the new era.

In April, May, June, and July, Venus spends an extended time in your house of siblings and writing. It is a great time for creative writing whether it is for a book, a business plan, press release, a grant proposal, academic article, or a memoir. It is also a great time to connect to relatives and find a neighbor who can become a good friend.

The eclipses this year continue to pit home and family opposite to career but, from around June, for the next year and a half, they will change signs and force you to face your truth as well as teach you to be authentic in your communication and businesses. The eclipses and North Node will ask you to focus on relatives, writing, change your communication infrastructure, as well as let go of any rigid dogma and / or philosophy you uphold. Since Chiron is still in your sign, take extra care of your body and health. Be careful of head injuries, over training, or accidents.

Those born between March 21 to 30 will experience Chiron stepping right on their Sun. This aspect can also manifest as a strong connection to a shaman or a spiritual teacher. You may feel you are stepping into the role of a teacher, healer, or consultant. However, Chiron conjunct your Sun can manifest as physical or emotional wounds.

The Six Eclipses
Your Emotional Landscape

In Part I, I shared the meaning behind the eclipses as well as their Sabian symbols and path. To make it easier, I have included some of that information below, as well as the way the eclipses manifest in your sign.

As a Fire-Bender, the eclipses in 2019 were not easy. They were "forcing" you to deal with deep seated emotions as well as confront parts of your personality you preferred to keep hidden. In addition, as a fellow cardinal (leader) sign, the eclipses in Cancer and Capricorn, "pushed" you into action but not always with a clear direction. However, in 2020, things are changing. The eclipses are moving to Gemini and Sagittarius which are far more compatible with your nature and alchemy. The eclipses will still be junctions for manifestation and generate change in your philosophy, education, communication, and contracts.

Jan 10 / 11: Penumbral Lunar eclipse in Cancer. Sabian symbol: Prima donna singing. Eclipse path: Europe, Asia, Australia, Africa, most of North America, eastern part of South America, Pacific, Atlantic, Indian Oceans.

To understand the story of this eclipse, let's return to the movie analogy. The first act of your story took place during the eclipses of July 2019. The eclipse of January 10, 2020, is the second act of your film. The third and final act is performed on the eclipse of July 5, 2020. Pay attention to synchronicities or anything out of the ordinary taking place during these dates and try to link the events of the eclipses to a narrative. The eclipses fall in your house of home and family as well as the house of career and therefore, you might feel a push and pull between these two aspects of your life. Your North Node in the house of home asks you to invest and focus on your home, real estate, family, and whatever makes you feel, rather than put too much emphasis on your career.

June 5 / 6: Penumbral Lunar eclipse in Sagittarius.
Sabian symbol: Seagulls watching a ship. Eclipse path: Europe, most of Asia, Australia, Africa, south / east South America, Pacific, Atlantic, Indian Oceans, Antarctica. This eclipse is the first of the new Gemini-Sagittarius axial eclipses.

Truth versus lies, authentic against fake. This eclipse is forcing you to focus on your message. What do you want to say? Who is your agent or messenger? To whom do you want to deliver the message? The North Node for the next 18 months will be asking you to focus on communication, contracts, business, connections, and relatives.

June 21: Solar Annular Solstice eclipse in Cancer.
Sabian symbol: A sailor ready to hoist a new flag to replace an old one.

Eclipse path: south / east Europe, most of Asia, North Australia, most of Africa, Pacific, and Indian Oceans. This eclipse is a big deal, especially if you are born between March 20-25. In addition, this eclipse takes place during a retrograde bonanza: Mercury, Venus, Pluto, Saturn, Pallas, and Jupiter are all in retrograde motion. This means their expression is more internal and it might feel like you are a passenger in a car driven by a very bad chauffeur. Take extra care of how you talk, relate, and communicate with lovers, friends, and authority figures. This is the last solar eclipse of Cancer that will square your tribe. The eclipse proposes a call for an action that is guided by an emotional component or relates to home and family. There could be a move, a change of location, or something new coming into your home or personal life.

July 4 / 5: Penumbral Lunar eclipse in Capricorn. Sabian symbol: An ancient bas-relief carved in granite. Eclipse path: south / west Europe, most of Africa, North America, South America, Pacific, Atlantic, and Indian Oceans, Antarctica. This eclipse is the mirror image of the Lunar eclipse of January 10 and therefore is the climax of whatever you started in July 2019. Mercury is retrograde during this eclipse, therefore we are still in danger of miscommunication and regretting our actions and / or choices. This eclipse once again pits home and security versus the need to make a jump or a change in your career. Uranus in your house of money is sending you a big electrical surge, something new and exciting can come out of something else ending.

Nov 29 / 30: Penumbral Lunar eclipse in Gemini. Sabian symbol: Quiver filled with arrows. Eclipse path: Europe, most of Asia, Australia, North America, South America, Pacific and Atlantic Oceans, Arctic. The eclipse continues the exploration of what is true and what is false. It is a time to change the way we learn and teach. There could be some conflict with in-laws or a pushback from people in authority. Be careful when traveling or in dealing with multinational corporations.

Dec 14: Total Solar eclipse in Sagittarius. Sabian symbol: Blue bird standing at the door of the house. Eclipse path: South Africa, South America, Pacific, Atlantic, and Indian Oceans, Antarctica. This is a powerful eclipse that begins a new journey in education, travel, and publishing. You might encounter an inspiring mentor or become one for someone else. There could be a new culture or country that excites you. In addition, there could be a new intellectual exploration or maybe a new language to learn.

Mercury Retrograde – *The Trickster*

Mercury is the trickster. Even when he is cruising direct through the heavens, he likes to pull practical jokes. I always thought that this was his compensation for delivering messages. When Mercury is retrograde, his tricks and ruses go to the next level. Of course, Mercury does not really retrograde, but from an earthly vantage point, Mercury does look as if he is going backwards three or four times a year for about three weeks. Mercury, the messenger of the gods and goddesses, represents the archetype of communication, connections, computers, emails, texts, messages, directions, information, data, cables, Wi-Fi, the nervous system, and breathing.

During Mercury retrograde, all these aspects of life are reversed, malfunctioning. Error messages, delays, accidents, mishaps, misspelling, and glitches plague the earth.

During Mercury retrograde, it is not recommended to start new long-term projects, sign documents, make large purchases, get married, start marketing campaigns, publish, inaugurate locations or homes, or release new products. Communications of all sorts are slower and more challenging. Computers crash; stock markets turn volatile; flights are delayed; traffic is worse than usual; accidents occur more often; and Murphy's Law takes hold of all aspects of our lives. If you need to fly during Mercury retrograde, make sure you do your online check-in and allow more time to reach the airport. Try to avoid overscheduling yourself or being overly critical and demanding. Also pay attention to your diet and food intake.

If you must start a new project, be as mindful as you can. Pay attention to small details and read in-between the lines if you must sign a document. Rewrite your emails; edit your texts; and think before you speak or post. In fact, it is better if you spend more time listening than talking. Life does not come to a halt during Mercury retrograde. You can still achieve a great deal during his retrograde. It is like going on a vacation in Sweden in the winter: It can still be fun, just make sure you take a coat. However, Mercury retrograde is a great time to edit, redo, reexamine yourself and your path, revisit old projects, and find lost objects. Try to focus on activities that have the prefix *re* – reevaluate, reedit, redo, reexamine, reconnect, regenerate, revisit, re-imagine, etc. Mercury is a liminal god and also a shadow-walker, a psychopomp, and a wizard (Hermetic studies are named after his Greek name).

Jung identified him as the god of synchronicities, and it is true that during Mercury retrograde there are far more synchronicities and meaningful coincidences. Yes, you might have made it to the wrong place for your meeting, but there you bump into someone you have been unable to track for ages. And yes, you might arrive to the appointment at 9 AM instead of 9 PM, but because of that "mistake" you avoided a terrible accident.

This year, the Mercury retrogrades are mostly swimming backwards in water signs, which for a Fire-Bender can be a bit challenging. Fire and water create a great deal of steam, which can manifest as over thinking.

1st Retro: February 16 – March 10. From Feb 16 to March 4 Mercury retrogrades in Pisces and falls in your house of letting go, mysticism, and past lifetimes. Be extra careful of escapist tendencies or falling prey to deceptions or addictions. But it can also manifest as synchronicities that bring you in contact with talents, skills, memories, and people you might have known in past lifetimes.

From March 4 to March 10, Mercury is retrograde in Aquarius, which is your house of government, friends, and community. You may have misunderstandings and / or issues with friends and / or people in your company.

2nd Retro: June 18 – July 12. Mercury retrogrades in Cancer. Be careful with this one, since it takes place during the powerful eclipse of the 21st of June. You can expect miscommunication with family members, real estate dealing, or anyone you consider familial. This can be a very emotional time for you with the eclipses and retrograde Mercury activating deep-core childhood issues.

3rd Retro: Oct 13 – Nov 3. Mercury is retrograde in Scorpio between October 13 and October 28, when Mars is also retrograde. This double-retro motion also happened in July and August 2018. You can go back and see what happened then and maybe avoid similar mistakes. Since Mars is your ruling planet and the ruler of Scorpio, where Mercury is now retrograde, you are in danger of acting or talking before thinking.

The fire and water combination is also not easy. So please take extra care during this retrograde. There could be issues with investments, death, taxes, production, and intimacy. From October 28 to November 3 Mercury will be retrograde in Libra, which falls in your house of relationships and partners. There could be some issues with lawsuits, or partners in work or in life.

Venus
Love, Pleasure, Art and Finance

Everyone loves Venus. Actually, what I just wrote, to an ancient Greek, would sound like a redundancy, since Venus embodies love and who does not love *love*? But this year, it will be harder to love love since Venus will be retrograding in Gemini between May 13 to June 25. She will be riding the Dragon, North Node, like an angry Khaleesi, who was just rejected by her John Snow. Venus goes retrograde once in 18 months for 40 days and 40 nights. It is a time we should dedicate to reevaluating our relationships, what we attract and what we are attracted to, how we relate to others, what talents we use to make money, as well as our core values and creeds. Some of us will have to confront insecurities and lower self-esteem during the retrograde. Many people change their attitudes, ideals, ethics, public image, dress code, and philosophies. It is a good time to get out of contracts that are not good for you.

Venus retrograde is a time when people are more blunt, combative, and lack diplomacy. You will also see a great deal of awkwardness on the world stage between diplomats as well as in the court system.

When Venus is retrograde, it is not recommended to get engaged or married, form business partnerships, buy art, make investments, start lawsuits, or spend money. If you are planning a cosmetic operation or an IVF, better wait for Venus to forget about her rejection and land her dragon safely on greener pastures.

Venus retrograde in Gemini specifically deals with how we communicate with our significant others, as well as relationships with business partners, siblings, and relatives. During Venus' long journey in Gemini (April 3 to August 7), we have the opportunity to connect beauty, art, and finance with communication, technology, and business. Letters merge with notes, numbers with colors. Your art can be communicative and your communication artistic.

The retrograde can bring back money that is owed to you as well as reconnect you with a talent or a project you have neglected in the past. You might also reconnect to a close friend from elementary or high school.

As an Aries, Venus retrograde takes place in your house of siblings and relatives, writing and communication. It is a good time to go back to an old business, writing project or an idea. There could be misunderstanding with a sibling or relative. So take it easy.

Venus is in Aries between February 7 and March 5. When Venus is in your sign, you feel attractive, desired, and lucky. You channel the qualities of beauty, diplomacy, and tact. You appear sympathetic, kind, and might even feel more flirtatious. Be careful not to overdo it and fall into vanity and largesse. However, since Venus is in your house of relatives and siblings for such a long time (April – early August), it means that these people can be helpful. In addition, you will find yourself as a hub, a connector, an agent to many people as well as connected to many new individuals. Writing of all kinds will be easier and beneficial this year.

Mars
Assertion, Passion, Leadership

Mars is the engine of the zodiac; he is hot, driven, passionate, aggressive, explosive, and impulsive. The Romans saw him as their father and some scholars trace his mythological origins as the god of vegetation. Mars is still associated with spring and seeds. Even in Genesis 1:12, we find a hint of the connection between Mars and vegetation. On the third day of creation, that is on "Martes" (day of Mars), God created vegetation and seeds: "Let the earth burst forth with every sort of grass and seed-bearing plant, and fruit trees with seeds inside the fruit, so that these seeds will produce the kinds of plants and fruits they came from." And so it was, and God was pleased.

Between June 28 and the end of the year, Mars will be traveling in Aries. This is abnormal as Mars usually spends about six weeks, not six months, in a sign. Mars, the god of war, is the ruler of Aries, the sign of warfare.

Yes, this can raise the probability of armed conflict, cyber-attacks, and other displays of aggression. This transit indicates there will be a great deal of strife, discord, and conflict. Astrology, like anything else in life, is relative — you might feel more belligerent than your usual self. Call it an Incredible-Hulk aspect: things, people, and situations will drive you MADDDDDD!
This year, Mars will be retrograde in Aries between September 9 and November 14. When Mars is retrograde, it is not a very auspicious time to start big projects with large investments. It is not a good time for surgery and medical procedures unless urgent. Neither is it recommended to start an intimate or sexual relationship. Avoid buying big machinery, making large investments, or starting wars or lawsuits. It is a more dangerous time, since wars, conflicts, explosions, and terror seem to follow Mars. After all, Mars' moons are called Phobos (fear) and Deimos (terror). If you need to fight, let the opponent fire the first bullet. Whoever starts a war with Mars retrograde, loses.
The Brexit referendum took place during Mars retrograde in Aquarius, the sign of government and community. And what happened right after? Oops, regret. What have we done? That is a typical Mars retrograde reaction. Another infamous example is the non-aggression treaty signed by Nazi Germany and the Soviets before WWII (Molotov-Ribbentrop).
It was also during a Mars retrograde station, which obviously did not last long. Even though Mars retrograde is not the same as Mercury retrograde, avoid signing treaties or agreements that deal with action,

wars, or campaigns. Be mindful of what you agree to do, what you promise to carry out, what you fight for, and what you are willing to do to satiate your passions. Mars retrograde is a good time to review your past strategies, rethink your battles and wars, change direction in leadership, and admit that you were wrong.

Take extra care between October 13 and November 4, since both Mars and Mercury are retrograde. Miscommunications and misunderstandings can easily flare into full-fledged wars.

Below is a list of Mars transits through the signs that can help you determine where to focus your energy.

However, remember that even the best fighters need a general. Make sure you pace yourself and control your inner warrior.

January 3 to February 16 – Mars in Sagittarius: This Mars transit gives you a good start to the year with energy and passion for travel, study, and a search for your true authenticity. You are channeling Indiana Jones, the happy-go-lucky adventurer. You crave action and novel explorations. Action comes from or through foreigners and education. Be careful of conflicts with in-laws.

February 16 to March 30 – Mars in Capricorn: Mars through the filter of Capricorn exhibits his best qualities. He is the trained martial artist fighting only when it is needed and he can easily win.

However, be aware that Mercury retrograde might slow things down. As an Aries, this transit is very helpful in making things happen, pushing forward projects that demand leadership and initiation.

Mars is now transiting in your house of career. You possess a force similar to that of a unified and disciplined army.

March 30 to May 13 – Mars in Aquarius: This is a good time to fight for your ideals, for your group and company, and come to the rescue of a friend in need. However, it can also create conflict with certain friends or people in your company. This transit takes place in your house of government, friends, and organization. Channel your energy to fight *for* instead of *with* your friends. It is a good time to focus on philanthropic work. Like Robin Hood, you require a beloved gang or group of friends to make a difference in the world. It is also a good time for freeing your body, mind, and soul. Any team or group activity, or sport is also recommended.

May 13 to June 28 – Mars in Pisces: With this transit of Mars, you have to make sure you are getting enough sleep and rest. Give time for your immune system to recover. It is a good time for interval fasting as well as for meditation and yoga. Two powerful eclipses as well as Venus retrograde are taking place and it can be intense out there. It is a good time for physical activities near or in water such as swimming, surfing, rowing, hiking / running / cycling by a body of water. This transit takes place in your house of letting go, so learn how to surrender without declaring defeat. You are regrouping, not retreating. Dreams and memories from past lives might become very intense in these six weeks. Take it easy during this transit.

June 29 – End of the Year – Mars in Aries: Mars likes to be home in Aries, the sign of his rulership. The king is back in his palace. However, it can get hot and aggressive. Mars in Aries can be domineering. So back off and don't be overly cocky or too pushy. Lead through example and not through fear or intimidation.

It is a good time to explore, do things you have never done, ask for a raise, and put your foot down about things that are important to you. However, remember that between September 9 and November 14, Mars is retrograde. Some delays and a pushback from life will take place. It might feel as if you are hitting the brakes after going 100 mph. This transit takes place in your first house, the house of identity and leadership. You will hear a call to action, feel a need to go on an adventure, to boldly go where no one has gone before. It is a time for pioneering. However, be careful from overtraining or stretching yourself too thin. You will be prone to accidents and or injuries. So be warned.

Uranus: *Unpredictability, Originality, and a Touch of* Chaos

In March 2019, Uranus made his final move into Taurus

and will stay there until 2026, falling in your house of finance, talents, and self-worth. Please pay attention to your financial situation the next few years. Uranus is called "the Joker" or "the Fool". He is chaotic but also ingenious. You might suddenly get an *aha* moment that can help your finances and give you an original idea or a bright inkling about your earning potential. Even if you cannot manifest the idea right now, write it down. In the future, you might have time and resources to make it happen. Uranus favors technology, innovation, and science. Maybe you can think of a great new application or an e-commerce business idea.

It is also a good time to redo your website, give your Facebook page a face-lift, and connect to social media.

Your Hebrew Letter & Tarot Card:

Since 2020 is the year of 22, below is the Major Arcana
card associated with your sign as well as the Hebrew
letter. You can use the letter and place it inside the
diamond in your meditation. The letter can also be used
like a talisman, to help you connect to your archetype.
You will notice that in many cases, the letter's shape
resembles its meaning. In my book *Cosmic Navigator*, you
can find more information about the connection between
the Hebrew letters and the zodiac signs.

Tarot: THE EMPEROR

Hebrew letter: Hey

ה

The letter means "a window." In Hebrew, the definite article (the prefix, Hey) is added to a word to make it definite. Aries does the same by being associated with the key words "I AM."

Summary:

2020 is an intense year that is filled with challenges and new beginnings which rise out of the ashes of the old. You will experience a great deal of change and transition in your career; at times, it will feel like the world is your oyster and other times you will feel like the world has abandoned you. However, the second part of the year brings a great deal of action and movement. Along with your ruler, Mars, you will be able to wake up and claim your place in the world.

TAURUS

New Karmic Cycle: *Mission Statement*

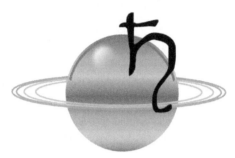

This year, you continue to dive deeper into your truth and authenticity. Every three decades, Saturn asks you to rewrite your constitution. To redefine and update your creed and philosophy. You are asked by the Lord Karma to decide what you believe in and what you are willing to fight for.

In 2020 your doctrine will be finalized and between March 16 – June 23, Saturn, the karmic teacher, moves into your house of career, taking all that you have learned in the last two years and implementing it in your vocation. From June 23 until mid-December, you will once again have to focus on learning and adjusting your philosophy so that in 2021-2023 you can once again mold your career according to your new outlook on life.

Taurus is a fixed earth sign and your job is to be a pillar, a support beam, a retaining wall, an Atlas that carries the weight of the world. But this year you will have to practice flexibility.

Since the end of 2017, Saturn has been transiting in Capricorn, a fellow earth sign. It allows you to maintain your posture and continue on your tracks, but in 2020, as Saturn moves into Aquarius, he will square your sign and cause change and a great need for flexibility and adjustment. To put it in simple words, in 2020 you need to focus on learning, teaching, and traveling for the purpose of preparing for a big change in your career that will start between mid-March until June 23 this year and throughout 2021 and 2022. You can travel back to 1991 and 1992 to learn the origin or roots of what is taking place in your career in 2020-2023. Saturn in the house of career is not only manifesting in your professional life, but it can also bring about synchronicities with father figures, bosses and authority figures. Saturn can also teach you lessons about how you function as a boss or a leader.

The greatest need for flexibility, however, is coming from Uranus. Since May of 2018, but more powerfully from March of 2019, Uranus, the planet of awakening and revolutions, moved into your sign for the first time in 84 years. This transit is very significant to all Tauruses but especially to those born between April 20-30 since Uranus will be conjunct your Sun in 2020.

Uranus in Taurus forces an awakening to all you bull-headed people. You will feel a need to rebel, to change and move. You might feel restless and impatient. It is as if you are a teenager again, wanting to break the old and reinvent the new.

Like anything in life, and therefore in astrology, it is futile to ask if it is a good or bad thing. While Uranus can be chaotic and disturbing, he can also provide an opportunity to dramatically change aspects of your life you are not happy about. You will also be funnier, more original, and innovative. It is as if Uranus is injecting you with extra IQ. Since Uranus is in your first house, try a new image. Change your style of dress. Try a new haircut, but also watch your body, and take care to avoid accidents and mishaps.

In 2020, Jupiter, the planet of luck and opportunities, blesses your travel and education. It is a great year to teach what you want to learn and learn what you want to teach. 2021 Jupiter will join Saturn and travel into your house of career, helping you manifest the changes you need to implement in order to be more successful.

In April, May, June, and July, Venus, your planet, will spend an extended time in your house of money, talents, and self-worth. This can be very helpful financially with new money-making ideas or new talents coming into the foreground. Expect a boost in your income.

The eclipse and conjunction in January falls in your house of travel, education, in-laws, justice, and truth. You will be tested, in a very practical way, on how true you are to your core beliefs. Avoid lies and be as authentic as you can.

Since Mars will be traveling for the last six months of the year in your house of hospitals and confinement, be extra careful with your actions. July – December can be a bit dangerous and you should avoid unnecessary conflicts, especially in September and October.

In general, 2020 promises a great deal of "roller-coaster" with constant sudden twists and changes. Try to be flexible mentally, emotionally, spiritually, and physically. Yes, that means compromise, some stretching and yoga, and a lot of meditation and sleep.

The Six Eclipses
Your Emotional Landscape

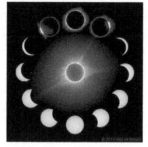

In Part I, I shared the meaning behind the eclipses as well as their Sabian symbols and paths. To make it easier, I have included some of that information below, as well as the way the eclipses manifest in your sign. The Moon, and all eclipses, have a very special relationship to you, Taurus. She is your best friend and is considered exalted when she transits in your sign. This year some of the eclipses (January 10, June 21, July 4) are in Cancer and Capricorn, water and earth signs that get along very well with you as you are an Earth-Bender. But from June, the North Node will move to your neighboring sign, Gemini, and well, you know, sometimes neighbors have issues. The eclipses at the end of the year will feel a bit more challenging and will deal with finance, death, and sexuality. You can go back to 2001 and 2002 to see how the eclipses in Gemini and Sagittarius worked with you in their last cycle.

Jan 10 / 11: Penumbral Lunar eclipse in Cancer. Sabian symbol: Prima donna singing. Eclipse path: Europe, Asia, Australia, Africa, most of North America, east part of South America, Pacific, Atlantic, and Indian Oceans.

To understand the story of this eclipse, let's return to the movie analogy. The first act of your story took place during the eclipses of July 2019. The eclipse of January 10, 2020, is the second act of your film. The third and final act is performed on the eclipse of July 5, 2020. Pay attention to synchronicities or anything out of the ordinary taking place during these dates and try to link the events of the eclipses to a narrative. The eclipses fall in your house of communication, relatives, business, commerce, and contracts. The eclipses bring about situations in which you will have to pay attention to how you communicate, what your message is, and who your audience is. It can also point at issues you have with relatives or the need to help or support them.

June 5 / 6: Penumbral Lunar eclipse in Sagittarius.
Sabian symbol: Seagulls watching a ship. Eclipse path: Europe, most of Asia, Australia, Africa, south / east South America, Pacific, Atlantic, Indian Oceans. This eclipse is the first of the new Gemini-Sagittarius axial eclipses. Truth versus lies, authentic against fake. This eclipse is pitting your finances against your partner's income. It is an opposition of mine-versus-ours or mine-versus-yours. The eclipse also can unveil issues in sexuality and intimacy as well as how you deal with death and letting go.

June 21: Solar Annular Solstice eclipse in Cancer.
Sabian symbol: A sailor ready to hoist a new flag to replace an old one. Eclipse path: south / east Europe, most of Asia, North Australia, most of Africa, Pacific, and Indian Oceans.

This eclipse takes place during a retrograde bonanza: Mercury, Venus, Pluto, Saturn, Pallas, and Jupiter are all in retrograde motion. This means their expression is more internal and it will feel like you are a passenger in a car driven by a very bad driver. Take extra care in how you relate to and communicate with lovers, friends, and figures of authorities. It is the last Solar eclipse of Cancer and marks a possibility for a new business, a renewed contract, a new connection in your life, maybe an agent or a mediator who helps you deal with past conflicts. It is a good time to change your attitude, thinking patterns, and how you relate to people. Be positive! **July 4 / 5: Penumbral Lunar eclipse in Capricorn.** Sabian symbol: An ancient bas-relief carved in granite. Eclipse path: south / west Europe, most of Africa, North America, South America, Pacific, Atlantic, and Indian Oceans. This eclipse is the mirror image of the Lunar eclipse of January 10 and therefore is the climax of whatever you started in July 2019.

Mercury is retrograde during this eclipse, therefore, we are still in danger of miscommunication and regretting our actions and / or choices. This eclipse once again can expose conflicts over finances between you and another person. It is a time to focus on your passions and what really drives you in life.

Nov 29 / 30: Penumbral Lunar eclipse in Gemini. Sabian symbol: Quiver filled with arrows. Eclipse path: Europe, most of Asia, Australia, North America, South America, Pacific, and Atlantic Oceans.

The eclipse continues the exploration of what is true and what is false. It is a time to change the way we learn and teach. This eclipse can unravel a hidden talent or gift that you might have neglected, which once developed, can bring a new source of income. In addition, insecurities and issues of self-wroth can manifest in your life.

Dec 14: Total Solar eclipse in Sagittarius. Sabian symbol: Blue bird standing at the door of the house. Eclipse path: South Africa, South America, Pacific, Atlantic, and Indian Oceans. This is a powerful eclipse that begins a new journey in education, travel, and publishing. You might encounter an inspiring mentor or become one for someone else. This solar eclipse could be the beginning of a new production, an arrival of an inheritance, or a return of a past investment. It is also a time you might feel your sexual drive rising. This eclipse can help you tap into your own healing abilities as well as find healing for yourself.

Mercury Retrograde - *The Trickster*

Mercury is the trickster. Even when he is cruising direct through the heavens, he likes to pull practical jokes. I always thought that this was his compensation for delivering messages. When Mercury is retrograde, his tricks and ruses go to the next level. Of course, Mercury does not really retrograde, but from an earthly vantage point, Mercury does look as if he is going backwards three or four times a year for about three weeks.

Mercury, the messenger of the gods and goddesses, represents the archetype of communication, connections, computers, emails, texts, messages, directions, information, data, cables, Wi-Fi, the nervous system, and breathing.

During Mercury retrograde, all these aspects of life are reversed, as in, malfunctioning. Error messages, delays, accidents, mishaps, misspellings, and glitches plague the earth.

During Mercury retrograde, it is not recommended to start new long-term projects, sign documents, make large purchases, get married, start marketing campaigns, publish, inaugurate locations or homes, or release new products. Communications of all sorts are slower and more challenging. Computers crash. Stock markets turn volatile; flights are delayed; traffic is worse than usual; accidents occur more often; and Murphy's Law takes hold of all aspects of our lives. If you need to fly during Mercury retro, make sure you do your online check-in and give yourself enough time to reach the airport. Try to avoid overscheduling yourself or being overly critical and demanding. Also, pay attention to your diet and food intake. If you must start a new project, be as mindful as you can. Pay attention to small details and read in-between the lines if you must sign a document. Rewrite your emails; edit your texts; and think before you speak or post. In fact, it is better if you spend more time listening than talking. Life does not come to a halt during Mercury retrograde. You can still achieve a great deal. It is like going on a vacation in Sweden in the winter: It can still be fun, just make sure you take a coat. However, Mercury retrograde is a great time to edit, redo, reexamine yourself and your path, revisit old projects, and find lost objects. Try to focus on activities that have the prefix *re* – reevaluate, reedit, redo, reexamine, reconnect, regenerate, revisit, re-imagine, etc. Mercury is a liminal god and also a shadow-walker, a psychopomp, and a wizard (Hermetic studies are named after his Greek name). Jung identified him as the god of synchronicities, and it is true that during Mercury retrograde there are far more synchronicities and meaningful coincidences. Yes, you might have made it to the wrong place for your meeting, but there you bump into someone you have been unable to track for ages. And yes, you might arrive to the appointment at 9 AM instead of 9 PM, but because of that "mistake" you avoided a terrible accident.

This year, the Mercury retrogrades are mostly swimming backwards in water signs which is great for you, Taurus, as an Earth-Bender. You are a tree and Mercury retrograde in water is like a gardener who forgot to turn off the hose. However, even trees can be overwatered and there is a bit of danger in being overly emotional or taking things too personally with the following Mercury retrogrades:

1st Retro: February 16 – March 10. From Feb 16 to March 4, Mercury retrogrades in Pisces and falls in your house of community, people, companies, and friends. There could be a great deal of misunderstanding within your company or organization, some challenges with friends, and maybe issues with governments (Did you pay your taxes?). From March 4 to March 10, Mercury retrograde in Aquarius, which is your house of career and father figures. Make sure you are extra careful dealing with authority figures, bosses, or your own father.

However, there could be inverted magic in your career, meaning something you didn't expect but have secretly wanted, might manifest.

2nd Retro: June 18 – July 12. Mercury retrogrades in Cancer. Be careful with this one, since it takes place during the powerful eclipse of the 21st of June. This retro falls in your house of communication and contracts, so make sure you don't sign any documents! This retrograde can also manifest as problems with neighbors, relatives, and siblings.

3rd Retro: Oct 13 – Nov 3. Mercury is retrograde in Scorpio between October 13 and October 28, when Mars is also retrograde. This double retro motion also happened in July and August 2018. You can look back and see what happened then and maybe avoid similar mistakes.

This retrograde is in your opposite sign, your mirror image — it is a bit more personal. You might have a distorted image of yourself or of how you communicate. For instance, you might think you have given a compliment, but it came across as a cynical remark, or it was perceived as criticism. From October 28 to November 3, Mercury will be retrograde in Libra, which falls in your house of health, diet, work, and routine. This retrograde can cause health issues and misunderstandings with employees or coworkers

Venus
Love, Pleasure, Art and Finance

Everyone loves Venus, your ruler. Actually, what I just wrote, to an ancient Greek, would sound like a redundancy, since Venus embodies love and who does not love *love*? Venus is your ruler, so she has a strong connection to you and your life. But this year, it will be harder to love love since Venus will be retrograding in Gemini between May 13 to June 25. She will be riding the Dragon, North Node, like an angry Khaleesi, who was just rejected by her John Snow. Venus goes retrograde once in 18 months for 40 days and 40 nights. It is a time we should dedicate to reevaluating our relationships, what we attract and what we are attracted to, how we relate to others, what talents we use to make money, as well as our core values and creeds. Some of us will have to confront insecurities and lower self-esteem during the retrograde.

Many people change their attitudes, ideals, ethics, public image, dress code, and philosophies. It is a good time to get out of contracts that are not good for you. Venus retrograde is a time when people are more blunt, combative, and lack diplomacy. You will also see a great deal of awkwardness on the world stage between diplomats as well as in the court system.

When Venus is retrograde, it is not recommended to get engaged or married, form business partnerships, buy art, make investments, start lawsuits, or spend money. If you are planning a cosmetic operation or an IVF, better wait for Venus to forget about her rejection and land her dragon safely on greener pastures.

Venus retrograde in Gemini specifically deals with how we communicate with our significant others, as well as relationships with business partners, siblings, and relatives. During Venus' long journey in Gemini (April 3 to August 7), we have the opportunity to connect beauty, art, and finance with communication, technology, and business. Letters merge with notes, numbers with colors. Your art can be communicative and your communication artistic.

The retrograde can bring back money owed to you and reconnect you with a talent or a project you have neglected in the past. You might also reconnect to a close friend from school.

Your sign is ruled by Venus, and therefore is far more connected to the synchronicities of Venus' transits. When Venus is retrograde in Gemini, she is in your house of finance and talents. She can bring talents you might have had when you were a teenager, or even earlier. Try to pursue them without thinking about whether it needs to involve a change of career. If you had a talent for ballet, join a dance class. If you played piano, reconnect to music. This aspect can also help you heal relationships with old flames, exes, as well as siblings and relatives. Venus is in Taurus between March 5 and April 3. When Venus is in your sign, you feel attractive, desired, and lucky. You channel the qualities of beauty, diplomacy, and tact. You appear sympathetic, kind, and might even feel more flirtatious. Be careful not to overdo it and fall into vanity and largesse. However, since Venus is in your house of money for such a long time (April – early August), it means that you can truly tap into your talents and increase your earning potential. The magic this year, brought by Venus, your ruler, is to connect to your self-worth. If you believe in yourself, so will the universe.

Mars
Assertion, Passion, Leadership

Mars is the engine of the zodiac; he is hot, driven, passionate, aggressive, explosive, and impulsive. The Romans saw him as their father and some scholars trace his mythological origins as the god of vegetation. Mars is still associated with spring and seeds. Even in Genesis 1:12, we find a hint of the connection between Mars and vegetation. On the third day of creation, that is on "Martes" (day of Mars), God created vegetation and seeds: "Let the earth burst forth with every sort of grass and seed-bearing plant, and fruit trees with seeds inside the fruit, so that these seeds will produce the kinds of plants and fruits they came from." And so it was, and God was pleased. Between June 28 and the end of the year, Mars will be traveling in Aries. This is abnormal as Mars usually spends about six weeks, not six months, in a sign. Mars, the god of war, is the ruler of Aries, the sign of warfare. Yes, this can raise the probability of armed conflict, cyber-attacks, and other displays of aggression. This transit indicates there will be a great deal of strife, discord, and conflict. Astrology, like anything else in life, is relative — you might feel more belligerent than your usual self. Call it an Incredible-Hulk aspect: things, people, and situations will drive you MADDDDDD! This year, Mars will be retrograde in Aries between September 9 and November 14. When Mars is retrograde, it is not a very auspicious time to start big projects with large investments. It is not a good time for surgery and medical procedures unless urgent. Neither is it recommended to start an intimate or sexual relationship. Avoid buying big machinery, making large investments, or starting wars or lawsuits. It is a more dangerous time, since wars, conflicts, explosions, and terror seem to follow Mars. After all, Mars' moons are called Phobos (fear) and Deimos (terror). If you need to fight, let the opponent fire the first bullet. Whoever starts a war with Mars retrograde, loses.

The Brexit referendum took place during Mars retrograde in Aquarius, the sign of government and community. And what happened right after? Oops, regret. What have we done? That is a typical Mars retrograde reaction. Another infamous example is the non-aggression treaty signed by Nazi Germany and the Soviets before WWII (Molotov-Ribbentrop). It was also during a Mars retrograde station, and, obviously did not last long.

Even though Mars retrograde is not the same as Mercury retrograde, avoid signing treaty or agreements that deal with action, wars, or campaigns. Be mindful of what you agree to do, what you promise to carry out, what you fight for, and what you are willing to do to satiate your passions. Mars retrograde is a good time to review your past strategies, rethink your battles and wars, change direction in leadership and admit that you were wrong. Take extra care between October 13 and November 4, since both Mars and Mercury are retrograde. Miscommunications and misunderstandings can easily flare into full-fledged wars.

Below is a list of Mars transits through the signs that can help you determine where to focus your energy. However, remember that even the best fighters need a general. Make sure you pace yourself and control your inner warrior.

January 3 to February 16 – Mars in Sagittarius. This Mars transit gives you a good start to the year with energy and passion for travel, study, and authenticity. Mars is driving full speed in your house of passion and sexuality. You will feel attractive and sexual. You will feel more energy to achieve your goals, especially if it relates to collaborating with other people's talents and money.

February 16 to March 30 – Mars in Capricorn. Mars through the filter of Capricorn exhibits his best qualities. He is the trained martial artist, fighting only when it is needed and when he can easily win. However, be aware that Mercury retrograde might slow things down. Mars is in your house of traveling, education, and in-laws. Be careful of unnecessary conflicts with your in-laws and take extra care if you need to travel abroad. But there could be action and movement in connection to foreign places that might feel familiar, as if you lived there in past lives. If you are physically active, this Mars transit is a good time to learn new exercise routine or train in a new way.

March 30 to May 13 – Mars in Aquarius: This is a good time to fight for your ideals, for your group and company, and come to the rescue of a friend in need. However, it can also create conflict with certain friends or people in your company. This transit takes place in your house of career and father figures. Be careful how you assert yourself with your superiors since you might feel invincible and overconfident. If you are self-employed or want to be, this is a good transit to initiate a project in your career or assume a leadership position.

May 13 to June 28 – Mars in Pisces: With this transit of Mars, you have to make sure you are getting enough sleep and rest. Give time for your immune system to recover. It is a good time for interval fasting as well as for meditation and yoga. Two powerful eclipses as well as Venus retrograde are taking place and it can be intense out there. It is a good time for physical activities near or in water
such as swimming, surfing, rowing, hiking / running / cycling by a body of water. This transit is taking place in your house of friends and companies. If you are working in a corporation or a large organization, there might be some power struggles and conflicts. However, it is also a good time to take charge, ask for a promotion, or push your agenda. You might be called to rescue a friend in need or fight for a close comrade.

June 29 – End of the Year – Mars in Aries: Mars likes to be home in Aries, the sign of his rulership. The king is back in his palace. However, it can get hot and aggressive. Mars in Aries can be domineering. So back off and don't be overly cocky or too pushy. Lead through example and not fear or intimidation. It is a good time to explore, do things you never did, ask for a raise, and put your foot down. However, remember that between September 9 and November 14, Mars is retrograde. Some delays and a pushback from life will take place. It might feel as if you are hitting the brakes after going 100 mph. Mars is traveling through your house of letting go, so don't be a stubborn bull. Learn how to surrender without declaring defeat. Learn how to recompose without retreat. Dreams and memories from past lives might become very intense in these six months. Take it easy during this transit as it can create conflicts that might make you feel jailed or isolated.

Uranus - *Unpredictability, Originality, and a Touch of Chaos*

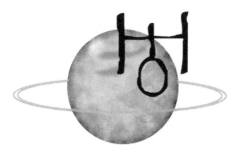

In March 2019, Uranus made his final move into your sign and will stay there until 2026, falling in your house of body, personality, and identity. There is no other way to interpret it: You are drastically and dramatically changing. This Uranus awakening takes place as Pluto and Saturn are sending you a great deal of help, especially if you are born in the last 10 days of Taurus (May 11-21). However, Uranus is unpredictable. So please don't take extra risks and be careful with your body. Humor can be a good way to deal with the new reality, especially towards the end of the year, since Uranus is, after all, dubbed "the Joker" or "the Fool". He is chaotic but also ingenious. You might suddenly get an *aha* moment that can help you in your awakening.

Uranus favors technology, innovation, and science. Maybe you can think of a great new application or an e-commerce business idea. Uranus in your sign is a good time to update and upgrade your computer, home, car, and your life in general. Try new things. Bring yourself up to date.

Your Hebrew Letter and Tarot Card:

Since 2020 is the year of 22, below is the Major Arcana card associated with your sign as well as the Hebrew letter. You can use the letter and place it inside the diamond in your meditation. The letter can also be used like a talisman to help you connect to your archetype. You will notice that in many cases, the letter's shape resembles its meaning. In my book *Cosmic Navigator*, you can find more information about the connection between the Hebrew letters and the zodiac signs.

Tarot: THE HIEROPHANT

Hebrew letter: Vav

וֹ

The letter means "a hook" or "nail." In Hebrew, the letter Vav is used as the conjunction "and." Like a nail it is supposed to put things together. Taurus is an earth sign that teaches us through the five senses to connect to the here and now.

Summary:

2020 is an intense year that is filled with challenges and new beginnings. There is a fresh new way of looking at life that changes your belief system, philosophy, education, as well as how you manage your life. You have to embrace that change, welcome it, replace the fear of the new with an excitement for that which is to be. The future is bright. Don't close your eyes.

.

GEMINI

New Karmic Cycle:
Sexuality, Passion, Transformation

This year, there is a lot to think about. The most important thing for a Gemini is that after 18-19 years, the North Node, the Dragon, is coming back to you. Dragons are reptiles that fly and since you are an air sign, you will experience a feeling of elevation. You will be able to cash in on good karma that you accumulated in the last two decades. All Geminis, but especially those born between June 11 – 21, will experience the flight of the dragon as the eclipses will pass close to your birthday. When the Dragon passes above your Sun, you become a Dragon. It is a year where you will form groups of like-minded people around you, join new communities, have more fans or followers, and digitally speaking, get more "likes" for your posts and social media activity, which I know is important to you. After all, you are the connector, you are the hub, the junction, the messenger. Since the North Node is in Gemini for the next 18 months, we are all asked to act, think, and communicate in a Gemini-like fashion. And who better to teach us how to deliver our messages than you, Gemini. You will notice that, especially from your birthday for the next 18 months, people will ask you for advice, counsel, ideas, and inspiration. Don't feel overwhelmed. You can do it. Saturn, the planet of karma and harsh lessons, is continuing his journey in your house of death and sexuality. Yes, there are some issues with your passion, drive, and intimacy. Saturn has been trying to fix it since the end of 2017 and this year you will have to graduate from these lessons. Having Saturn in the house of death can feel dark. You are going through a death of your old self and a rebirth of a new one. From middle of March until the end of June, Saturn will move into your house of travel and publishing (where he will also be in 2021 and 2022). During these times you will start to feel the resurrection. But then, from July to December this year, you will again have to deal with Lady Death and allow the final letting go. But no worries. You will fully resurrect at the end of the year. The peak of the challenges take place in January with the triple conjunction taking place in your house of death. Let it go, as one song says. Let it be, as another one suggests. Venus will spend a long time in your sign this year (April – early August). That is a great thing for your tribe. You will feel artistic, attractive, and get a boost in your income. However, she also retrogrades in your sign between May 13 and June 28, covering all Gemini birthdays. That means: surprise! Maybe an ex will show up to your birthday party like an uninvited witch or warlock. Try not to start any new relationships during the retrograde.

Uranus in your house of past lives might ask you to let go of things unexpectedly. Together with Saturn, Jupiter, and Pluto in your house of death and transformation, you cannot avoid the need to shed some layers and peel off your armor. You are forced to go deeper, and I am talking Dead-Sea deep, or Basso-Serio operatic voice deep. I know you don't always like to dive deep. After all, you are an air sign and prefer to scratch the surface so you can move faster from one topic to the other. But in 2020, your cycles are synchronized with the need to go explore the depth of your true self as well as your shadow. Even Jupiter, the planet of positivity, is in your house of death and transformation this year. You are learning to be a healer, a shaman, an investigator. There could be good news about investments and inheritances, and your partner in life or work might start making more money.

The Six Eclipses
Your Emotional Landscape

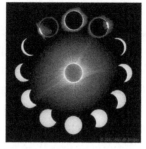

In Part I, I shared the meaning behind the eclipses as well as their Sabian symbols and paths. To make it easier, I have included some of that information below, as well as the way the eclipses manifest in your sign. As I mentioned before, the North Node, which always points at the location of the eclipses, is moving into Gemini in June, around your birthday. The last time the Dragon was in Gemini was October 2001 — May 2003. You can go back to these dates to see what happened in your life then. It is like a cycle repeating, but now you are equipped with an extra 19 years of wisdom and experience.

Jan 10 / 11: Penumbral Lunar eclipse in Cancer. Sabian symbol: Prima donna singing. Eclipse path: Europe, Asia, Australia, Africa, most of North America, east part of South America, Pacific, Atlantic, and Indian Oceans. To understand the story of this eclipse, let's return to the movie analogy. The first act of your story took place during the eclipses of July 2019. The eclipse of January

10, 2020, is the second act of your film. The third and final act is performed on the eclipse of July 5, 2020. Pay attention to synchronicities or anything out of the ordinary taking place during these dates and try to link the events of the eclipses to a narrative. The eclipses fall in your house of money, talent, and self-worth, and also the house of death and transformation where Saturn, Pluto, and Jupiter are already lurking. The eclipses can create an opposition between your income and your partner's finances. You might feel possessive or experience someone else's obsession. The eclipses can also feel like a time for dealing with death and separation.

June 5 / 6: Penumbral Lunar eclipse in Sagittarius.
Sabian symbol: Seagulls watching a ship. Eclipse path: Europe, most of Asia, Australia, Africa, south / east South America, Pacific, Atlantic, Indian Oceans. This eclipse is the first of the new Gemini-Sagittarius axial eclipses. Truth versus lies, authentic against fake. This is the first eclipse that is generated by the North Node transit into your sign. The eclipses create oppositions between you and your partners, either in work or in life. Events around partnership, law, justice, and enemies might come to the foreground.

June 21: Solar Annular Solstice eclipse in Cancer.
Sabian symbol: A sailor ready to hoist a new flag to replace an old one. Eclipse path: south / east Europe, most of Asia, north Australia, most of Africa, Pacific, and Indian Oceans. In addition, this eclipse takes place during a retrograde bonanza: Mercury, Venus, Pluto,

Saturn, Pallas, and Jupiter are all in retrograde motion. This means their expression is more internal and it will feel like you are a passenger in a car driven by a very bad driver. Take extra care of how you talk, relate, and communicate with lovers, friends, and figures of authorities. It is the last solar eclipse of Cancer and marks a possibility for a new beginning in your house of finance. Maybe a talent resurfaces that could potentially increase your income.

July 4 / 5: Penumbral Lunar eclipse in Capricorn. Sabian symbol: An ancient bas-relief carved in granite. Eclipse path: south / west Europe, most of Africa, North America, South America, Pacific, Atlantic, and Indian Oceans. This eclipse is the mirror image of the Lunar eclipse of January 10 and is therefore the climax of whatever you started in July 2019. Mercury is retrograde during this eclipse, therefore we are still in danger of miscommunication and regretting our actions and / or choices. This eclipse can expose conflicts over finances between your money and other people's money, as well as having to deal with letting go, issues around sexuality, and intimacy.

Nov 29 / 30: Penumbral Lunar eclipse in Gemini. Sabian symbol: Quiver filled with arrows. Eclipse path: Europe, most of Asia, Australia, North America, South America, Pacific and Atlantic Oceans. The eclipse continues the exploration of what is true and what is false. It is a time to change the way we learn and teach. The Moon is in your first house and the Sun is in the house of your partner. You might have a reversed gender role with your partner for a few days. If you are a woman, you might act more masculine and if you are a man, you will connect more to your femininity. This eclipse might feel especially volatile and emotional, so cut your partner some slack.

Dec 14: Total Solar eclipse in Sagittarius. Sabian symbol: Blue bird standing at the door of the house. Eclipse path: South Africa, South America, Pacific, Atlantic, and Indian Oceans. This is a powerful eclipse that begins a new journey in education, travel, and publishing. You might encounter an inspiring mentor or become one for someone else. This eclipse can jumpstart a new relationship or give you clarity about a relationship that exists.

Mercury Retrograde – *The Trickster*

Mercury, the ruler of your sign, is the trickster. Even when he is cruising direct through the heavens, he likes to pull practical jokes. When he is retrograde, his tricks go to the next level. Of course, Mercury does not really retrograde, but from an earthly vantage point, Mercury does look like he is going backwards three or four times a year for about three weeks.

Since Mercury, the messenger of the gods and goddesses, represents the archetype of communication, connections, computers, emails, texts, messages, directions, information, data, cables, Wi-Fi, the nervous system, and breathing, during Mercury retrograde, all these aspects of life are reversed, that is, malfunctioning: error messages, delays, accidents, mishaps, misspelling, and glitches are a few of these plagues.

 During Mercury retrograde, it is not recommended to start new long-term projects, sign documents, make

large purchases, get married, start marketing campaigns, publish, inaugurate, or release new products. Communications of all sorts are slower and more challenging. Computers crash; stock markets turn volatile; flights are delayed; traffic is worse than usual; accidents occur more often; and Murphy's Law takes hold of all aspects of our lives. If you need to fly during Mercury retrograde, make sure you do your online check-in and allow more time to reach the airport. Try to avoid overscheduling yourself or being overly critical and demanding. Also pay attention to your diet and food intake.

If you must start a new project, be as mindful as you can. Pay attention to small details and read in-between the lines if you must sign a document. Rewrite your emails; edit your texts; and think before you speak or post. In fact, it is better if you spend more time listening than talking. Life does not come to a halt during Mercury retrograde. You can still achieve a great deal during his retrograde. It is like going on a vacation in Sweden in the winter: It can still be fun, just make sure you take a coat However, it is a great time to edit, redo, reexamine yourself and your path, revisit old projects, and find lost objects. Try to focus on activities that have the prefix *re* – reevaluate, reedit, redo, reexamine, reconnect, regenerate, revisit, re-imagine, etc.

Mercury is a liminal god in that he is a shadow-walker, a psychopomp, and a wizard (Hermetic studies are named after his Greek name). Jung identified him as the god of synchronicities, and it is true that during Mercury retrograde there are far more synchronicities and meaningful coincidences. Yes, you might have made it to the wrong place for your meeting, but there you bump into someone you have been unable to track for ages. And yes, you might arrive to the appointment at 9 AM instead of 9 PM, but because of that "mistake," you avoided a terrible accident.

Mercury retrogrades always triggers more stories and mishaps for you, Gemini, since he is your ruler. In 2020, the Mercury retrogrades are mainly in water signs. You might feel overly emotional and will tend to take things very personally as you are an Air-Bender and don't always work well with water.

1st Retro: February 16 – March 10. From Feb 16 to March 4, Mercury retrogrades in Pisces and falls in your house of career. Please pay attention to how you communicate in your professional life and / or with bosses and father figures. From March 4 to March 10, Mercury is retrograde in Aquarius, which is your house of travel and education. Since it is also the house of truth, you might be prone to bending the truth, so take heed. This retrograde can also be synchronized with concerns about travel abroad, multinational organizations, or learning and teaching.

2nd Retro: June 18 – July 12. Mercury retrograde in Cancer. Be careful with this one, since it takes place during the powerful eclipse on June 21st. This retrograde falls in your house of money and talents. Make sure you don't make any serious investments, purchases, or other financial commitments. Even without these activities, there might be unexpected financial upsets.

3rd Retro: Oct 13 – Nov 3. Mercury is retrograde in Scorpio between October 13 and October 28, when Mars is also retrograde. This double-retro motion also happened in July and August 2018. You can go back and see what happened then and maybe avoid similar mistakes. This retrograde takes place in your house of health, work and diet. Be extra strict with your routine since that can help ride this retrograde out. There might be a bit of difficulty with your health but also with employees and co-workers. From October 28 to November 3 Mercury will be retrograde in Libra, which falls in your house of love, happiness, and children. If you have kids, they might drive you crazy. If you have a secret love affair, come clean or be extra careful.

Venus
Love, Pleasure, Art and Finance

Everyone loves Venus. Actually, what I just wrote, to an ancient Greek, would sound like a redundancy, since Venus embodies love and who does not love *love*?
But this year, it will be harder to love love, since Venus will be retrograding in Gemini between May 13 and June 25. She will be riding the Dragon, North Node, like an angry Khaleesi, who was just rejected by her John Snow. Venus goes retrograde once in 18 months for 40 days and 40 nights. It is a time we should dedicate to reevaluating our relationships, what we attract and what we are attracted to, how we relate to others, what talents we use to make money as well as our core values and creeds. Some of us will have to confront insecurities and lower self-esteem during the retrograde.

Many people change their attitudes, ideals, ethics, public image, dress code, and philosophies. It is a good time to get out of contracts that are not good for you. Venus retrograde is a time when people are more blunt, combative, and lack diplomacy. You will also see a great deal of awkwardness on the world stage between diplomats as well as the court system.

When Venus is retrograde, it is not recommended to get engaged or married, form business partnerships, buy art, make investments, start lawsuits, or spend money. If you are planning a cosmetic operation or an IVF, better wait for Venus to forget about her rejection and land her dragon safely on greener pastures.

Venus retrograde in Gemini specifically deals with how we communicate with our significant others, as well as relationships with business partners, siblings, and relatives. During Venus' long journey in Gemini (April 3 to August 7), we have the opportunity to connect beauty, art and finance with communication, technology, and business. Letters merge with notes, numbers with colors. Your art can be communicative and your communication artistic. The retrograde can bring back money owed to you and reconnect you with a talent or a project you have neglected in the past. You might also reconnect to a close friend from school.

It is not every year — or even every few years — that Venus decides to settle in your sign for such a long period of time. She likes to be in Gemini, she can be the socialite and the influencer she craves to be while she travels in your communicative sign. During Venus retrograde, you should go to a vintage clothes store. Who knows? Maybe you will pick up something you used to wear.

Venus is in your sign for a long time in 2020: April 3 to August 7. When Venus is in your sign, you feel attractive, desired, and lucky. You channel the qualities of beauty, diplomacy, and tact. You appear sympathetic, kind, and might even feel more flirtatious.

Mars
Assertion, Passion, Leadership

Mars is the engine of the zodiac; he is hot, driven, passionate, aggressive, explosive, and impulsive. The Romans saw him as their father and some scholars trace his mythological origins as a god of vegetation. Mars is still associated with spring and seeds. Even in Genesis 1:12, we find a hint of the connection between Mars and vegetation. On the third day of creation, that is on "Martes" (day of Mars), God created vegetation and seeds: "Let the earth burst forth with every sort of grass and seed-bearing plant, and fruit trees with seeds inside the fruit, so that these seeds will produce the kinds of plants and fruits they came from." And so it was, and God was pleased.

Between June 28 and the end of the year, Mars will be traveling in Aries. This is abnormal as Mars usually spends about six weeks, not six months, in a sign. Mars, the god of war, is the ruler of Aries, the sign of warfare. Yes, this can raise the probability of armed conflict, cyber-attacks, and other displays of aggression.

This transit indicates there will be a great deal of strife, discord, and conflict. Astrology, like anything else in life is relative. So, you might feel more belligerent relative to your regular self. Call it an Incredible-Hulk aspect: things, people, and situations will drive you MADDDDDD!

This year, Mars will be retrograde in Aries between September 9 and November 14. When Mars is retrograde, it is not a very auspicious time to start big projects with large investments. It is not a good time for surgery and medical procedures unless urgent. Neither is it recommended to start an intimate or sexual relationship. Avoid buying big machinery, making large investments, or starting wars or lawsuits. It is a more dangerous time. Since wars, conflicts, explosions, and terror seem to follow Mars. After all, Mars' moons are called Phobos (fear) and Deimos (terror). If you need to fight, let the opponent fire the first bullet. Whoever starts a war with Mars retrograde, loses.

The Brexit referendum took place during Mars retrograde in Aquarius, the sign of government and community. And what happened right after? Oops, regret. What have we done? That is a typical Mars retrograde reaction. Another infamous example is the non-aggression treaty signed by Nazi Germany and the Soviets before WWII (Molotov-Ribbentrop). It was also during a Mars retrograde station, and, obviously did not last long. Even though Mars retrograde is not the same as Mercury retrograde, avoid signing treaties or agreements that deal with action, wars, or campaigns. Be mindful of what you agree to do, what you promise to carry out, what you fight for, and what you are willing to do to satiate your passions. Mars retrograde is a good time to review your past strategies, rethink your battles and wars, change direction in leadership, and admit that you were wrong. Take extra care between October 13 and November 4, since both Mars and Mercury are retrograde. Miscommunications and misunderstandings can easily flare into full-fledged wars.

Below is a list of Mars' transits through the signs that can help you determine where to focus your energy. However, remember that even the best fighters need a general. Make sure you pace yourself and control your inner warrior.

January 3 to February 16 – Mars in Sagittarius: This Mars transit gives you a good start of the year with energy and passion for travel, study, and authenticity. Mars is driving full speed in your house of relationships. This could manifest as conflict but also passion in relationships. This position of Mars can also manifest as issues with enemies and lawsuits. Choose your battles wisely. **February 16 to March 30 – Mars in Capricorn:** Mars through the filter of Capricorn exhibits his best qualities. He is the trained martial artist, fighting only when needed and when he can easily win. However, be aware that Mercury retrograde might slow things down.

Mars is racing through your house of passion and sexuality. You will feel attractive and sexual. You will feel more energy to achieve your goals, especially if it relates to collaborating with other people's talents and money.

March 30 to May 13 – Mars in Aquarius: This is a good time to fight for your ideals, for your group and company, and come to the rescue of a friend in need. However, it can also create conflict with certain friends or people in your company. Mars is in your house of traveling, learning, and in-laws. Be careful of unnecessary conflicts with your in-laws or with foreigners. But there could be action and movement in connection to foreign places that might feel familiar, as if you lived there in past lives. If you are physically active, this Mars transit is a good time to learn new exercise routines or train in a new way.

May 13 to June 28 – Mars in Pisces: With this transit of Mars, you have to make sure you are getting enough sleep and rest. Give time for your immune system to recover. It is a good time for interval fasting as well as for meditation and yoga. Two powerful eclipses, as well as Venus retrograde, are taking place and it can be intense out there. It is a good time for physical activities near or in water such as swimming, surfing, rowing, hiking / running / cycling by a body of water. This transit takes place in your house of career and father figures.

Be careful how you assert yourself with your superiors, since you might feel invincible and overconfident. If you are self-employed or want to be, this is a good transit to initiate a project in your career or assume a leadership position.

June 29 – End of the Year – Mars in Aries: Mars likes to be home in Aries, the sign of his rulership. The king is back in his palace. However, it can get hot and aggressive. Mars in Aries can be domineering. So back off and don't be overly cocky or too pushy. Lead through example and not fear or intimidation. It is a good time to explore, do things you never did, ask for a raise, and put your foot down. However, remember that between September 9 and November 14, Mars is retrograde. Some delays and a pushback from life will take place. It might feel as if you are hitting the brakes after going 100 mph. This transit is taking place in your house of friends and companies. If you are working in a corporation or a large organization, there might be some power struggles and conflict. However, it is also a good time to take charge, ask for a promotion, and push your agenda. You might be called to rescue a friend in need or fight for a close comrade. Since Mars will be in Aries for so long, it could also manifest as an appearance of a brother- or sister-in-arms, or a new cause to fight for on behalf of other people.

Uranus - *Unpredictability, Originality, and a Touch of Chaos*

In March 2019, Uranus made his final move into Taurus and will stay there until 2026, falling in your house of past lifetimes, hospitals, mysticism, confinements, jails, retreat, and suffering. That sounds worse than it is, but it is a warning that things can suddenly disappear from your life and you will suddenly be asked to let go of things that you might have thought were important. This aspect happens once every 84 years, it is rare and therefore enduring.

Uranus is also dubbed "the Joker" or "the Fool". He is chaotic but also ingenious. You might suddenly get an *aha* moment that can help you awaken. Since Uranus is traveling in your house of past lives, you might all of a sudden encounter a skill or ability you possessed in a past lifetime.

Many meetings with people or locations you visit will appear familiar from previous lives. Your psychic abilities and intuition will also increase as well as wild lucid and sci-fi dreams.

Uranus favors technology, innovation, and science. Maybe you can think of a great new application or an e-commerce business idea.

Your Hebrew Letter and Tarot Card:

Since 2020 is the year of 22, below is the Major Arcana card associated with your sign as well as the Hebrew letter. You can use the letter and place it inside the diamond in your meditation. The letter can also be used like a talisman to help you connect to your archetype. You will notice that, in many cases, the letter's shape resembles its meaning. In my book *Cosmic Navigator*, you can find more information about the connection between the Hebrew letters and the zodiac signs.

Tarot: THE LOVERS

Hebrew letter: Zain

ז

The letter means "a sword." The sword, intellectually speaking, is associated with the tongue, hence language, the domain of Gemini. Sharp intellect, can be as deadly as a sharp blade.

Summary:

2020 is an intense year that is filled with magical journeys into the Underworld, past lifetimes, and your subconscious. You will deal with a great amount of transformation but also experience a powerful new awakening. During this year you will also be able to harvest the benefits from all the good deeds you have accomplished in the last 19 years.

.

CANCER

New Karmic Cycle:
Relationships and Partnership

2020 is an intense and powerful year for the Cancer clan. From November 2018 until June 2020, the North Node or Dragon, is surfing in your sign. The last time this happened was 2000 and 2001. The North Node in Cancer helped us assume the qualities of your sign: unconditional love, compassion, home, family, and security. This North Node transit in Cancer put you on the spotlight as we look up to you to show us the way. In June the North Node will move to Gemini and travel into your house of past lives, mysticism, and letting go. Since the North Node shows us what our soul desires (not what our ego wants), this means that for the next 18 months you have to practice surrender (not defeat), letting go, empathy, and meditation. This transit asks you to connect to your intuition, trust your psychic abilities, and work with the suffering of other people. Every once and a while, spend time alone so you can cleanse yourself from other people's influences and expectations.

In 2020, there is a great deal of activity in Capricorn, your opposite and complimentary sign. Pluto, Saturn, and Jupiter are in Capricorn and transit your house of relationships. Saturn has been in your house of relationships since the end of 2017 and manifested as focus and challenges in your major relationships in life or in business. Saturn is never easy and many of you Cancerians got married or divorced. Saturn in your house of relationships encourages you to make serious decisions and commitment in all your partnerships. This year, Jupiter joins Saturn in your house of relationship, which is great news. It feels like in the last two years you asked a lot of questions about relationships and now Jupiter comes to give some answers and bring some flow. Many of you will get married, engaged, sign partnership agreements and find favorable resolution in lawsuits. The Pluto-Saturn conjunction in January 2020 can be very transformative, and you will have to make tough decisions about your partners in work and in life. It could also mean that your partner is going through a difficult time. Make sure to be there for them with your natural empathy, but also make sure to place boundaries. From mid-March to end of June, Saturn, the planet of karma, will move into Aquarius and into your house of death and transformation. You can expect a big shift in your life and the beginning of a two-year journey into the Underworld.

The last time Saturn was in your house of death, sexuality, and transformation was in 1991-1993. In 2021 and 2022, Saturn will return to the house of death, completing the sheading of whatever you carry that is not needed for your transformation. When Saturn is in your house of death and sexuality, you are asked to look deeper into your passions; work with other people's money and their talents (production, banking, management), as well as peeling away whatever is not needed. Along with the North Node in the house of letting go, these next two years present a great period for letting go of whatever prevents you from assuming your true potential.

The eclipses in January and June will be very powerful for you as they are in Cancer and fall in your house of body and identity, as well as the house of relationships. You can expect the drama of July 2019 to continue into 2020 with some resolution around the Solstice of June 21. Mars plows through your house of career for the last six months of the year, giving you a push towards leadership as well as the potential for initiating and spearheading new projects. Be extra careful from September — October not to overextend yourself or your authority, and avoid unnecessary conflicts with people in authority or bosses.

In April, May, June, and July, Venus spends an extended time in your house of past lifetimes and imagination. This can prove to be a very creative period with memories, images, as well as subliminal skills and talents resurfacing. Maybe a lover or a close friend from a past lifetime will return to your life. Be open — but then again Cancer — you always are.

The Six Eclipses
Your Emotional Landscape

In Part I, I shared the meaning behind the eclipses as well as their Sabian symbols and paths. To make it easier, I have included some of that information below, as well as the way the eclipses manifest in your sign. Eclipses are always very powerful for you no matter where they fall since the Moon is the ruler of your sign. As I mentioned earlier, the eclipses have been in Cancer since the end of 2018, and you have felt as if you are driving in turbo mode. This year, the eclipses are shifting to Gemini and it can feel like a relief. While you like to take care of things, it can be taxing to take care of a cranky Moon-mama. Let the twins deal with the sometimes-bad-tempered mother. This year, until 2022, the eclipses are in your house of karma, previous lives, and mysticism. This indicates that memories from past lives, dreams, and mystical experiences are important for the next 18 months, and that there will be a great deal of letting go in your life.

Make sure to start a meditation or yoga practice to help channel these vibrations.

Jan 10 / 11: Penumbral Lunar eclipse in Cancer. Sabian symbol: Prima donna singing. Eclipse path: Europe, Asia, Australia, Africa, most of North America, eastern part of South America, Pacific, Atlantic, Indian Oceans. To understand the story of this eclipse, let's return to the movie analogy. The first act of your story took place during the eclipses in July 2019. The eclipse of January 10, 2020 is the second act of your film. The third and final act is performed on the eclipse of July 4, 2020. Pay attention to synchronicities or anything out of the ordinary taking place during these dates and try to link the events of the eclipses to a narrative. The eclipses fall in your first house of body, personality, and direction. You are pushed by the eclipses into making decisions about your direction in life as well as the trajectory of your relationships. The eclipse pits you versus your partners, your needs against your partners' needs. Since the North Node is in your first house, make sure you are putting yourself first BUT don't be selfish.

June 5 / 6: Penumbral Lunar eclipse in Sagittarius. Sabian symbol: Seagulls watching a ship. Eclipse path: Europe, most of Asia, Australia, Africa, south / east South America, Pacific, Atlantic, Indian Oceans. This eclipse is the first of the new Gemini-Sagittarius axial eclipses. Truth versus lies, authentic against fake. This eclipse is forcing you to focus on your health, work, diet, routine, and service. There is a part of you that wants to disappear and a part that wants to be engaged and offer help, service, and support. Make sure you are being authentic in your work. If you don't let your kids drink Coca-Cola, don't apply for a job as a marketing director in that firm.

June 21: Solar Annular Solstice eclipse in Cancer.
Sabian symbol: A sailor ready to hoist a new flag to replace an old one. Eclipse path: south / east Europe, most of Asia, North Australia, most of Africa, Pacific, and Indian Oceans. In addition, this eclipse takes place during a retrograde bonanza: Mercury, Venus, Pluto, Saturn, Pallas, and Jupiter are all in retrograde motion. This means their expression is more internal and it will feel like you are a passenger in a car driven by a very bad driver. Take extra care to how you talk, relate, and communicate with lovers, friends, and authority figures. It is the last solar eclipse of your sign and will give you a last big push forward, setting you on a new direction. This eclipse is like a pathfinder, helping you rebrand yourself and initiate a new image.

July 4 / 5: Penumbral Lunar eclipse in Capricorn. Sabian symbol: An ancient bas-relief carved in granite. Eclipse path: south / west Europe, most of Africa, North America, South America, Pacific, Atlantic, and Indian Oceans.

This eclipse is the mirror image of the Lunar eclipse of January 10 and is also the climax of whatever you started in July 2019. Mercury is retrograde during this eclipse; therefore we are still in danger of miscommunication and regretting our actions and / or choices. This eclipse once again pits you versus a partner or significant other. Be extra careful with lawsuits or any needless conflicts.

Nov 29 / 30: Penumbral Lunar eclipse in Gemini. Sabian symbol: Quiver filled with arrows. Eclipse path: Europe, most of Asia, Australia, North America, South America, Pacific, and Atlantic Oceans. The eclipse continues the exploration of what is true and what is false. It is a time to change the way we learn and teach. This eclipse can manifest as changes in work or a need to let go of some aspect of your professional life. A coworker or employee might go through some challenges or pose some threat to you.

Dec 14: Total Solar eclipse in Sagittarius. Sabian symbol: Blue bird standing at the door of the house. Eclipse path: South Africa, South America, Pacific, Atlantic, Indian Oceans.

This is a powerful eclipse that begins a new journey in education, travel, and publishing. You might encounter an inspiring mentor or become one for someone else. This is a good time to start a new job, a new diet, or embark on a healthier routine.

Mercury Retrograde - *The Trickster*

Mercury is the trickster. Even when he is cruising direct through the heavens, he likes to pull practical jokes. I always thought that this was his compensation for delivering messages. When Mercury is retrograde, his tricks and ruses go to the next level. Of course, Mercury does not really retrograde, but from an earthly vantage point, Mercury does look as if he is going backwards three or four times a year for about three weeks. Mercury, the messenger of the gods and goddesses, represents the archetype of communication, connections, computers, emails, texts, messages, directions, information, data, cables, Wi-Fi, the nervous system, and breathing. During Mercury retrograde, all these aspects of life are reversed, malfunctioning. Error messages, delays, accidents, mishaps, misspelling, and glitches plague the earth.

During Mercury retrograde, it is not recommended to start new long-term projects, sign documents, make large purchases, get married, start marketing campaigns, publish, inaugurate locations or homes, or release new products. Communications of all sorts are slower and more challenging. Computers crash; stock markets turn volatile; flights are delayed; traffic is worse than usual; accidents occur more often; and Murphy's Law takes hold of all aspects of our lives. If you need to fly during Mercury retrograde, make sure you do your online check-in and allow more time to reach the airport. Try to avoid overscheduling yourself or being overly critical and demanding. Also pay attention to your diet and food intake.

If you must start a new project, be as mindful as you can. Pay attention to small details and read in-between the lines if you must sign a document. Rewrite your emails; edit your texts; and think before you speak or post. In fact, it is better if you spend more time listening than talking. Life does not come to a halt during Mercury retrograde. You can still achieve a great deal during his retrograde. It is like going on a vacation in Sweden in the winter: It can still be fun, just make sure you take a coat. However, Mercury retrograde is a great time to edit, redo, reexamine yourself and your path, revisit old projects, and find lost objects. Try to focus on activities that have the prefix *re* – reevaluate, reedit, redo, reexamine, reconnect, regenerate, revisit, re-imagine, etc.

Mercury is a liminal god and also a shadow-walker, a psychopomp, and a wizard (Hermetic studies are named after his Greek name). Jung identified him as the god of synchronicities, and it is true that during Mercury retrograde there are far more synchronicities and meaningful coincidences. Yes, you might have made it to the wrong place for your meeting, but there you bump into someone you have been unable to track for ages. And yes, you might arrive at the appointment at 9 AM instead of 9 PM but, because of that "mistake," you may have avoided a terrible accident.

This year, the Mercury retrogrades are mostly swimming backwards in water signs, which is perfect for you as a Water-Bender. This means you may be able to benefit from these retrogrades. Just be extra cautious between June 18 and July 12, when Mercury retrogrades in your sign.

1st Retro: February 16 – March 10. From Feb 16 to March 4, Mercury retrogrades in Pisces and falls in your house of travel, education, and truth. Be careful not to bend the truth, even if you are trying to avoid hurting someone's feelings. If you are traveling abroad, make sure you pay attention to details such as flight times and changes, visa rules, etc. From March 4 to March 10, Mercury is retrograde in Aquarius, your house of death and transformation. This can be a bad time for investments as well as miscommunication with people in your intimate life.

2nd Retro: June 18 – July 12. Mercury retrogrades in Cancer. Be careful with this one since it takes place during the powerful eclipse of the 21st of June. You can expect miscommunication with family members, real estate, or anyone you consider familial. This retrograde can be extra hard on your body so make sure to boost your immune system and be careful to avoid accidents.

3rd Retro: Oct 13 – Nov 3. Mercury is retrograde in Scorpio between October 13 and October 28, when Mars is also retrograde. This double retro motion also happened in July and August 2018. You can go back and see what happened then and try to avoid similar mistakes. This retrograde falls in your house of children, love, and happiness. There may be some issues with your kids or with their schedules; this retrograde might also manifest as misunderstandings or problems with lovers. From October 28 to November 3 Mercury will be retrograde in Libra, which may cause challenges with family members and real estate.

Venus
Love, Pleasure, Art and Finance

Everyone loves Venus. Actually, what I just wrote, to an
ancient Greek, would sound like a redundancy, since
Venus embodies love and who does not love *love*?
But this year, it will be harder to love *love* since Venus
will be retrograding in Gemini between May 13 to June
25. She will be riding the Dragon, North Node, like an
angry Khaleesi, who was just rejected by her John Snow.
Venus goes retrograde once in 18 months for 40 days and
40 nights. It is a time we should dedicate to reevaluating
our relationships, what we attract and what we are
attracted to, how we relate to others, what talents we use
to make money, as well as our core values and creeds.
Some of us will have to confront insecurities and lower
self-esteem during the retrograde.

Many people change their attitudes, ideals, ethics, public
image, dress code, and philosophies. It is a good time to
get out of contracts that are not good for you. Venus
retrograde is a time when people are more blunt,
combative, and lack diplomacy. You will also see a great
deal of awkwardness on the world stage between
diplomats as well as the court system.

When Venus is retrograde, it is not recommended to get engaged or married, form business partnerships, buy art, make investments, start lawsuits, or spend money. If you are planning a cosmetic operation or an IVF, better wait for Venus to forget about her rejection and land her dragon safely on greener pastures.

Venus retrograde in Gemini specifically deals with how we communicate with our significant others, as well as relationships with business partners, siblings, and relatives. During Venus' long journey in Gemini (April 3 to August 7), we have the opportunity to connect beauty, art, and finance with communication, technology, and business. Letters merge with notes, numbers with colors. Your art can be communicative and your communication artistic.

The retrograde can bring back money owed to you and reconnect you with a talent or a project you have neglected in the past. You might also reconnect to a close friend from school.

As a Cancer, Venus retrograde takes place in your house of past lives and letting go. You may experience fights or even breakups with partners or lovers. An ex-lover or an old flame you might have known in a past life, or in this one, might return. It can be a time for creativity and projects that require originality and imagination.

Venus is in your sign between August 7 and September 6 and you feel attractive, desired, and lucky. You channel the qualities of beauty, diplomacy, and tact. You appear sympathetic, kind, and might even feel more flirtatious. Be careful not to overdo it and fall into vanity and largesse. However, since Venus is in your house of karma, past lifetimes, and intuition (April – early August), you might feel this year that help comes from within, from developing and trusting your intuition and . . . imaginary friends.

Mars
Assertion, Passion, Leadership

Mars is the engine of the zodiac. He is hot, driven, passionate, aggressive, explosive, and impulsive. He was named "Father of Rome" and he might have had his origins as the god of vegetation. Mars is still associated with spring and seeds. Even in Genesis 1:12, we find a trace of the connection between Mars and vegetation. On the third day of creation, that is on "Martes" (day of Mars), God created vegetation and seeds, which is something on which monotheists and pagans agree.

This year, Mars will be traveling from June 28 until the end of the year in Aries, although he usually spends just a few weeks in a sign. Mars, the god of war, is the ruler of Aries, the sign of warfare. This does not necessarily mean war is upon us, but it surely does indicate there will be a great deal of strife, discord, and conflict. Astrology, like anything else in life is relative — and you might feel more belligerent than your usual self. Call it an Incredible-Hulk aspect: things, people, situations will drive us MADDDDDD!

This year, Mars will be retrograde in Aries between September 9 to November 14. When Mars is retrograde, it is not a very auspicious time to start big projects with large investments. It is not a good time for surgery and medical procedures. Neither is it recommended to start an intimate or sexual relationship. Avoid buying big machinery, making large investments, or starting wars or lawsuits. It is a more dangerous time, since wars, conflicts, explosions, and terror seem to follow Mars. After all, Mars' moons are called Phobos (fear) and Deimos (terror). If you need to fight, let the opponent fire the first bullet. Whoever starts a war with Mars retrograde, loses.

The Brexit referendum took place during Mars retrograde in Aquarius, the sign of government and community. And what happened right after? Oops, regret. What have we done? That is a typical Mars retrograde reaction. Another infamous example is the non-aggression treaty signed by Nazi Germany and the Soviets before WWII (Molotov-Ribbentrop). It was also a Mars retrograde station, and, obviously the treaty did not last long. Watch out for what agreements or treaties you sign, what you agree to, what you promise to do, what you fight for, and what you are willing to do to satiate your passions. Mars retrograde is a good time to review your past strategies, rethink your battles and wars, change direction in leadership, and admit that you were wrong. Take extra care between October 13 and November 4, since both Mars and Mercury are retrograde. Miscommunications and misunderstandings can easily flare into full-fledged wars.

Below is a list of Mars transits through the signs that can help you determine where to focus your energy. However, remember that even the best fighters need a general. Make sure you pace yourself and control your inner warrior.

January 3 to February 16 – Mars in Sagittarius: This Mars transit gives you a good start to the year with energy and passion for travel, study, and authenticity. Mars is plowing through your house of health, diet, and work. It is a good time to start a new exercise routine, initiate a new project at work, fight for a promotion, or explore new leadership roles in your workplace. Don't wait for things to happen. Make them manifest! Watch your health, head injuries as well as other accidents. Mars in this house can manifest as conflicts with employees and coworkers.

February 16 to March 30 – Mars in Capricorn: Mars through the filter of Capricorn exhibits his best qualities. He is the trained martial artist, fighting only when it is needed and when he can easily win. However, be aware that Mercury retrograde might slow things down. Since Mars will join Saturn, Jupiter, and Pluto in your house of relationships and partnership, it means that in these six weeks there could be a great deal of either conflict or energy around your significant others. Be careful of enemies and antagonists and choose your battles wisely. Any sport or physical activity done in partnership is favored.

March 30 to May 13 – Mars in Aquarius: This is a good time to fight for your ideals, for your group and company and come to the rescue of a friend in need. However, it can also create conflict with certain friends or people in your company. This transit of Mars can help connect you to your passion and sexuality, as well as to your life force. This happens with Saturn is in the same house — karma and action unite. Joint artistic and financial affairs might require you to take a leadership role.

May 13 to June 28 – Mars in Pisces: With this transit of Mars, you have to make sure you are getting enough sleep and rest. Give time for your immune system to recover. It is a good time for interval fasting as well as for meditation and yoga. Two powerful eclipses, as well as Venus retrograde, are taking place and it can be intense out there. It is a good time for physical activities near or in water such as swimming, surfing, rowing, hiking / running / cycling by a body of water. This is a good time for travel, especially travel that involves adventures. However, be careful of conflict with teachers, mentors, in-laws, and foreigners.

June 29 – End of the Year – Mars in Aries: Mars likes to be home in Aries, the sign of his rulership. The king is back in his palace. However, it can get hot and aggressive. Mars in Aries can be domineering. So back off and don't be overly cocky or too pushy. Lead through example and not fear or intimidation. It is a good time to explore, to do things you have never done, to ask for a raise or put your foot down.

However, remember that between September 9 and November 14, Mars is retrograde. Some delays and a pushback from life will take place. It might feel as if you are hitting the brakes after going 100 mph. This transit is a bit more challenging as Aries is square to your sign and can create conflict and feelings of stress. This transit takes place in your career and can manifest as conflict with father figures or superiors in work. However, you can use this time to assert your leadership abilities and take actions towards achieving your goals.

Uranus - *Unpredictability, Originality, and a Touch of Chaos*

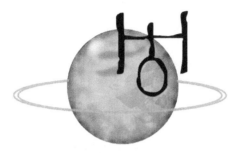

In March 2019, Uranus made his final move into Taurus and will stay there until 2026. This falls in your house of community, friends, and organizations and you are bound to makes changes in your groups of friends, surroundings, clubs, and companies. New people will storm into your life and become best friends, while others will disappear with similar speed. There might be some sudden issues with the government or a changes of leadership in your company.

Uranus is called "the Joker" or "the Fool". He is chaotic but also ingenious. You might suddenly get an *aha* moment that can help your position in your company or corporation. You might find funny, unique and ingenious new friends, or your older friends might see a hilarious new you.

Uranus favors technology, innovation, and science. Maybe you can think of a great new application or an e-commerce business idea. It is also a good time to redo your website, give your Facebook page a face lift, and connect to social media. You will find yourself joining new virtual communities or joining new social media platforms.

Your Hebrew Letter and Tarot Card:

Since 2020 is the year of 22, below is the Major Arcana card associated with your sign as well as the Hebrew letter. You can use the letter and place it inside the diamond in your meditation. The letter can also be used like a talisman to help you connect to your archetype. You will notice that in many cases, the letter's shape resembles its meaning. In my book *Cosmic Navigator*, you can find more information about the connection between the Hebrew letters and the zodiac signs.

Tarot: THE CHARIOT

Hebrew letter: Chet

ח

The letter means "a wall." The wall is a symbol of the protection of the home, the shell of the hermit crab, as well as the womb.

Summary:

2020 is an intense year that is filled with challenges and emotional periods (especially January, June and December). Your main focus this year is fixing your relationships, breaking patterns in your partnership and attracting the right people into your life. 2020 is a year when you begin a two-and-a-half-year process of major transition and change which will allow you to connect to your power and tap your full potential.

LEO

New Karmic Cycle:
Work, Service, Health

2020 continues and deepens your search for your mission in life. With the cluster of planets settling in your house of work and service, it is a once-in-a-three-decade opportunity to learn how to serve others and find your true calling. I know you might be raising eyebrows, thinking "Me? Serving?" Yes, the royals of the zodiac need to learn how to serve. Every good king and queen in history will tell you that they served their people and, in turn, the people served them.

The last two years have been somewhat difficult with work, employees, health, and diet since Saturn, the Lord Karma, has been scrutinizing these aspects of your life. Since the end of 2017, there have been a great deal of changes and extra responsibilities in your work and / or health. There could have been some issues with coworkers or employees.

Major changes in work and routine started in 2008 when Pluto moved into your house of work, and it felt even heavier with Saturn joining in 2018.

The good news is that this year you have Jupiter, the planet of luck and flow, entering the house of work and health and this should herald good news, a chance for healing, and maybe a promotion.

However, watch your health as well as work in January with the eclipses and the big conjunction, forcing monumental pressure in your routine and work. To sum it up, 2020 is the year you learn how to serve others (work), how to serve your body (diet), how your body serves you (health), how people serve you (employees, coworkers), as well as how time serves you (routine). These are the main questions to be answered in the next 12 months.

The eclipses this year are in your house of health, work, and service as well as the house of mysticism and letting go. The eclipses in January and July are forcing you to confront these issues and therefore, preventive medicine, changing your diet, being patient at work, and allowing change to happen without resistance can facilitate the transition. 2020 gives you a once in almost 30 years opportunity to create the work environment and career that you need. You can build your kingdom this year. Supporting this trend is the fact that Uranus is now officially in your house of career. Uranus brings awakenings, unexpected change and the need to update and upgrade your vocation. It started in 2019 and will continue until 2026. There will be sudden twists and turns, so hold on and welcome the original and the new. If you have a boss or have to deal with father figures, Uranus can also manifest as craziness and chaos with superiors. Make sure not to explode or lose your cool.

The last six months of the year places a great deal of focus on travel, education, and truth, as Mars will plow through your house of foreign cultures and authenticity. Mars will challenge you to fight for what you believe in, to walk the talk, and to be true to your creed. July to December are good months to initiate projects abroad or embark on an intellectual journey that might include learning a new language, higher-education, or simply educating yourself about a subject of interest. There could be some conflict and quarrels with in-laws, especially in September and October.

Venus' long journey in your house of friends, between April and early August, presents possibilities to join new companies, make new friends, and reconnect to people you might have lost contact within the last decade.

In mid-May until July, Saturn changes gear and moves into your house of relationships and partnerships. This aspect can create some breathing space in your work and some good news about health, but it forces you to look deep into all of your contractual relationships and partnerships.

Saturn will return to that house in 2021 and 2022 and you will be focused less on work and professional life, and more on your personal life.

The Six Eclipses
Your Emotional Landscape

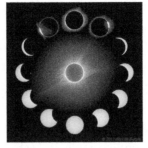

In Part I, I shared the meaning behind the eclipses as well as their Sabian symbols and paths. To make it easier, I have included some of that information below, as well as the way the eclipses manifest in your sign. Eclipses, especially Solar eclipses, are not easy for you to handle. The Sun is your ruler and during the Solar eclipses (June 21 and December 14), the Moon blocks the Sun's rays from reaching your mane. However, when the North Node moves into Gemini (June 2020 – December 2021) the eclipses will be easier for you to handle.

Jan 10 / 11: Penumbral Lunar eclipse in Cancer. Sabian symbol: Prima donna singing. Eclipse path: Europe, Asia, Australia, Africa, most of North America, east part of South America. Pacific, Atlantic, and Indian Oceans. To understand the story of this eclipse, let's return to the movie analogy. The first act of your story took place during the eclipses of July 2019.

The January 10, 2020 eclipse is the second act of your film. The third and final act is performed on the eclipse of July 5, 2020. Pay attention to synchronicities or anything out of the ordinary taking place during these dates and try to link the events of the eclipses to a narrative. The eclipses fall in your house of past lifetimes, hospitals, jails, suffering, and mysticism. This eclipse is asking you to let go, surrender (without defeat), relax, and focus on meditation. The eclipse can also ask you to let go of some aspects in your work or diet that do not serve you well.

June 5 / 6: Penumbral Lunar eclipse in Sagittarius.
Sabian symbol: Seagulls watching a ship. Eclipse path: Europe, most of Asia, Australia, Africa, south / east South America, Pacific, Atlantic, Indian Oceans. This eclipse is the first of the new Gemini-Sagittarius axial eclipses. Truth versus lies, authentic against fake. This eclipse is a shift of focus and energy. The Moon and Sun are opposite and pulling and pushing you between the houses of love and friends. If you have children, there could be some issues surfacing with them or they might be going through some challenges. The eclipse also can cause an opposition between a lover and a friend or a friend who turns into a lover. However, it is a very creative eclipse that can help you let go of whatever prevents your happiness.

June 21: Solar Annular Solstice eclipse in Cancer.
Sabian symbol: A sailor ready to hoist a new flag to replace an old one. Eclipse path: south / east Europe, most of Asia, North Australia, most of Africa, Pacific, and Indian Oceans. In addition, this eclipse takes place during a retrograde bonanza: Mercury, Venus, Pluto,

Saturn, Pallas, and Jupiter are all in retrograde motion. This means their expression is more internal and it will feel like you are a passenger in a car driven by a very bad driver. Take extra care of how you talk, relate, and communicate with lovers, friends, and authority figures. This Solar eclipse is emotional and can be a bit dangerous as it falls in your house of undoing and hospitals. Be extra careful and mindful of your health. However, the eclipse can help you start a new mystical journey or meditation routine, or give you a glimpse of talents and skills you had in past lives that could serve you well in your present lifetime.

July 4 / 5: Penumbral Lunar eclipse in Capricorn. Sabian symbol: An ancient bas-relief carved in granite. Eclipse path: south / west Europe, most of Africa, North America, South America, Pacific, Atlantic, and Indian Oceans. This eclipse is the mirror image of the Lunar eclipse of January 10 and therefore is the climax of whatever you started in July 2019.

Mercury is retrograde during this eclipse, therefore we are still in danger of miscommunication and regretting our actions and / or choices. There could be emotional situations in work or regarding your health. Make sure you don't medicate yourself with drugs, sugar, or carbs. Again, there is a need to let go of something in order to have more success at work. It is also a good time for imaginative and creative projects.

Nov 29 / 30: Penumbral Lunar eclipse in Gemini. Sabian symbol: Quiver filled with arrows. Eclipse path: Europe, most of Asia, Australia, North America, South America, Pacific and Atlantic Oceans. The eclipse continues the exploration of what is true and what is false. It is a time to change the way we learn and teach. This eclipse asks you to look deeply into what makes you happy, and see how you can tap into the creative forces in your life.

Dec 14: Total Solar eclipse in Sagittarius. Sabian symbol: Blue bird standing at the door of the house. Eclipse path: South Africa, South America, Pacific, Atlantic and Indian Oceans. This is a powerful eclipse that begins a new journey in education, travel, and publishing. You might encounter an inspiring mentor or become one for someone else. Love and creativity, fun, and happiness can be the gifts of this eclipse. It is also a new beginning for your inner child, and a great time to start a hobby, sport, or a recreation activity.

Mercury Retrograde - *The Trickster*

Mercury is the trickster. Even when he is cruising direct through the heavens, he likes to pull practical jokes. I always thought that this was his compensation for delivering messages. When Mercury is retrograde, his tricks and ruses go to the next level. Of course, Mercury does not really retrograde, but from an earthly vantage point, Mercury does look as if he is going backwards three or four times a year for about three weeks. Mercury, the messenger of the gods and goddesses, represents the archetype of communication, connections, computers, emails, texts, messages, directions, information, data, cables, Wi-Fi, the nervous system, and breathing. During Mercury retrograde, all these aspects of life are reversed, malfunctioning. Error messages, delays, accidents, mishaps, misspelling, and glitches plague the earth.

During Mercury retrograde it is not recommended to start new long-term projects, sign documents, make large purchases, get married, start marketing campaigns, publish, inaugurate locations or homes, or release new products. Communications of all sorts are slower and more challenging. Computers crash; stock markets turn volatile, flights are delayed, traffic is worse than usual; accidents occur more often; and Murphy's Law takes hold of all aspects of our lives. If you need to fly during Mercury retrograde, make sure you do your online check-in and allow more time to reach the airport. Try to avoid overscheduling yourself or being overly critical and demanding. Also pay attention to your diet and food intake.

If you must start a new project, be as mindful as you can. Pay attention to small details and read in-between the lines if you must sign a document. Rewrite your emails; edit your texts; and think before you speak or post. In fact, it is better if you spend more time listening than talking. Life does not come to a halt during Mercury retrograde. You can still achieve a great deal during his retrograde. It is like going on a vacation in Sweden in the winter: It can still be fun, just make sure you take a coat. However, Mercury retrograde is a great time to edit, redo, reexamine yourself and your path, revisit old projects, and find lost objects. Try to focus on activities that have the prefix *re* – reevaluate, reedit, redo, reexamine, reconnect, regenerate, revisit, re-imagine, etc.

Mercury is a liminal god and also a shadow-walker, a psychopomp, and a wizard (Hermetic studies are named after his Greek name). Jung identified him as the god of synchronicities, and it is true that during Mercury retrograde there are far more synchronicities and meaningful coincidences. Yes, you might have made it to the wrong place for your meeting, but there you bump into someone you have been unable to track/find for ages. And yes, you might arrive at the appointment at 9 AM instead of 9 PM, but because of that "mistake," you avoided a terrible accident.

This year, the Mercury retrogrades are mostly swimming backwards in water signs, which is not easy for you as a Fire-Bender. The retrogrades could be like a firehose trying to extinguish your flames. That is why it might feel more emotional and frustrating. No roaring or exposing your fangs.

1st Retro: February 16 – March 10. From Feb 16 to March 4, Mercury retrogrades in Pisces and falls in your house of intimacy, sexuality, production, investments, and death. Ok, it sounds worse than it is, but yes, it is intense. There could be some money owed returning to you but also miscommunications with the people closest to you. If you have a secret love affair, well, be extra careful or cut it off. From March 4 to March 10, Mercury is retrograde in Aquarius, your house of relationships and partnerships — this retrograde is very personal as it involves partners in life or in work. Be careful of enemies and lawsuits.

2nd Retro: June 18 – July 12. Mercury retrogrades in Cancer. Be careful with this one, since it takes place during the powerful eclipse of the 21st of June. Mercury is creating the perfect scenario for a past lifetime regression. Mercury is retrograde in your house of past lives, addictions, lack of boundaries, and confinements. Make sure to not put yourself in some sort of mental or emotional jail. However, your meditations, recollections of previous lives, and intuition can be very high.

3rd Retro: Oct 13 – Nov 3. Mercury is retrograde in Scorpio between October 13 and October 28, when Mars is also retrograde. This double retro motion also happened in July and August 2018. You can go back and see what happened then and maybe avoid similar mistakes. This retrograde falls in your house of home and family. There could be misunderstandings with family members, or concerning land and real estate. From October 28 to November 3 Mercury will be retrograde in Libra which falls smack in your house of communication — it is a double retrograde. Be careful not to sign anything and there could be some challenges with relatives and siblings.

Venus
Love, Pleasure, Art and Finance

Everyone loves Venus. Actually, what I just wrote, to an ancient Greek, would sound like a redundancy, since Venus embodies love and who does not love *love*?

But this year, it will be harder to love *love*, since Venus will be retrograding in Gemini between May 13 to June 25. She will be riding the Dragon, North Node, like an angry Khaleesi, who was just rejected by her John Snow. Venus goes retrograde once in 18 months for 40 days and 40 nights. It is a time we should dedicate to reevaluating our relationships, what we attract and what we are attracted to, how we relate to others, what talents we use to make money, as well as our core values and creeds. Some of us will have to confront insecurities and lower self-esteem during the retrograde. Many people change their attitudes, ideals, ethics, public image, dress code, and philosophies. It is a good time to get out of contracts that are not good for you.

Venus retrograde is a time when people are more blunt, combative, and lack diplomacy. You will also see a great deal of awkwardness on the world stage between diplomats as well as in the court system.

When Venus is retrograde, it is not recommended to get engaged or married, form business partnerships, buy art, make investments, start lawsuits, or spend money. If you are planning a cosmetic operation or an IVF, better wait for Venus to forget about her rejection and land her dragon safely on greener pastures.

Venus retrograde in Gemini specifically deals with how we communicate with our significant others, as well as relationships with business partners, siblings, and relatives. During Venus' long journey in Gemini (April 3 to August 7), we have the opportunity to connect beauty, art, and finance with communication, technology, and business. Letters merge with notes, numbers with colors. Your art can be communicative and your communication artistic.

The retrograde can bring back money owed to you and reconnect you with a talent or a project you have neglected in the past. You might also reconnect to a close friend from school.

As a Leo, Venus retrograde takes place in your house of friends, groups, and organizations. Friends from the distant past might reconnect, or even long-lost flames be reignited. A friend might become a romantic partner, but also a current romance might transform into a friendship.

Old creative or artistic projects might spark a renewed interest.

From September 6 to October 2, Venus is in your sign. You feel attractive, desired, and lucky. You channel the qualities of beauty, diplomacy, and tact. You appear sympathetic, kind, and might even feel more flirtatious. Be careful not to overdo it and fall into vanity and largesse. However, since Venus is in your house of friends (April – early August) this year, friends and colleagues may end up being your saviors, helping you tap into your talent and finance as well as present opportunities to make you feel better about yourself and your work.

Mars
Assertion, Passion, Leadership

Mars is the engine of the zodiac. He is hot, driven, passionate, aggressive, explosive, and impulsive. The Romans saw him as their father and some scholars trace his mythological origins as a god of vegetation. Mars is still associated with spring and seeds. Even in Genesis 1:12, we find a hint of the connection between Mars and vegetation. On the third day of creation, that is on "Martes" (day of Mars), God created vegetation and seeds: "Let the earth burst forth with every sort of grass and seed-bearing plant, and fruit trees with seeds inside the fruit, so that these seeds will produce the kinds of plants and fruits they came from." And so it was, and God was pleased.

Between June 28 and the end of the year, Mars will be traveling in Aries. This is abnormal as usually Mars spends about six weeks, not six months, in a sign. Mars, the god of war, is the ruler of Aries, the sign of warfare. Yes, this can raise the probability of armed conflict, cyber-attacks, and other displays of aggression.

This transit indicates there will be a great deal of strife, discord, and conflict. Astrology, like anything else in life is relative and you might feel more belligerent than your usual self. Call it an Incredible-Hulk aspect: things, people, and situations will drive you MADDDDDD! This year, Mars will be retrograde in Aries between September 9 to November 14. When Mars is retrograde, it is not a very auspicious time to start big projects with large investments. It is not a good time for surgery and medical procedures unless urgent. Neither is it recommended to start an intimate or sexual relationship. Avoid buying big machinery, making large investments, or starting wars or lawsuits. It is a more dangerous time, since wars, conflicts, explosions, and terror seem to follow Mars. After all, Mars' moons are called Phobos (fear) and Deimos (terror). If you need to fight, let the opponent fire the first bullet. Whoever starts a war with Mars retrograde, loses.

The Brexit referendum took place during Mars retrograde in Aquarius, the sign of government and community. And what happened right after? Oops, regret. What have we done? That is a typical Mars retrograde reaction. Another infamous example is the non-aggression treaty signed by Nazi Germany and the Soviets before WWII (Molotov-Ribbentrop). It was also a Mars retrograde station, and, obviously the treaty did not last long.

Even though Mars retrograde is not the same as Mercury retrograde, avoid signing treaties or agreements that deal with action, wars, or campaigns. Be mindful of what you agree to do, what you promise to carry out, what you fight for, and what you are willing to do to satiate your passions. Mars retrograde is a good time to review your past strategies, rethink your battles and wars, change direction in leadership, and admit that you were wrong.

Take extra care between October 13 and November 4, since both Mars and Mercury are retrograde. Miscommunications and misunderstandings can easily flare into full-fledged wars.

Below is a list of Mars transits through the signs that can help you determine where to focus your energy.

However, remember that even the best fighters need a general. Make sure you pace yourself and control your inner warrior.

January 3 to February 16 – Mars in Sagittarius: This Mars transit gives you a good start to the year with energy and passion for travel, study, and authenticity. Mars is plowing through your house of children, love, and happiness which for a Leo, it is not too bad of a placement. Mars wants you to be active, entertaining, and fun. Spend time outdoors and initiate recreational activities. We all want to enjoy the childlike (not childish) qualities that we love you for. This is also a good time for a creative project or a new hobby.

February 16 to March 30 – Mars in Capricorn: Mars, through the filter of Capricorn, exhibits his best qualities. He is the trained martial artist, fighting only when it is needed and he can easily win. However, be aware that Mercury retrograde might slow things down. Mars is in your house of diet, health, and work. It is a good time to start a new exercise routine, initiate a project in work, fight for a promotion, or explore leadership roles in your workplace. Don't wait for things to happen. Make them manifest! Watch your health, head injuries as well as accidents. Mars in this house can manifest as conflicts with employees and coworkers.

March 30 to May 13 – Mars in Aquarius: This is a good time to fight for your ideals, for your group and company, and come to the rescue of a friend in need. However, it can also create conflict with certain friends or people in your company. Since Mars is in your house of relationships and partnership, it means that in these six weeks there could be a great deal of either conflict or energy around your significant others. Be careful of enemies and choose your battles wisely. Any sport or physical activity done in partnership is favored. **May 13 to June 28 – Mars in Pisces:** With this transit of Mars, you have to make sure you are getting enough sleep and rest. Give time for your immune system to recover.

It is a good time for interval fasting as well as for meditation and yoga. Two powerful eclipses, as well as Venus retrograde are taking place and it can be intense out there. It is a good time for physical activities near or in water such as swimming, surfing, rowing, hiking / running / cycling by a body of water. This transit of Mars can help connect you to your passion and sexuality as well as to your life force. Joint artistic and financial affairs might force you to take a leadership role.

June 29 – End of the Year – Mars in Aries: Mars likes to be home in Aries, the sign of his rulership. The king is back in his palace. However, it can get hot and aggressive. Mars in Aries can be domineering. So back off and don't be overly cocky or too pushy. Lead through example and not fear or intimidation. It is a good time to explore, do things you never did, ask for a raise, and put your foot down. However, remember that between September 9 and November 14, Mars is retrograde. Some delays and a pushback from life will take place. It might feel as if you are hitting the brakes after going 100 mph. This is a good time for travel, especially journeys that include adventures and / or education. However, be careful of conflict with teachers, mentors, in-laws, and foreigners. It is a time to fight for what you believe in and believe in what you fight for. Your philosophies might be challenged but hold on to your truth.

Uranus - *Unpredictability, Originality, and a Touch of Chaos*

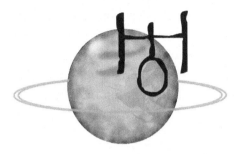

In March 2019, Uranus made his final move into Taurus, which is located in your house of career, and will stay there until 2026. Change is bound to happen in your professional life, as well as some awakening to the true nature of your path in life. What is your purpose in this life? How do you want to contribute to humanity? Uranus in your house of career is asking you to think more altruistically, more globally and universally. Uranus feeds off originality and innovation. This is a great opportunity to shake up your career, adding an element of community, technology, and a jump into something you never done before.

Uranus is called "the Joker" or "the Fool". He is chaotic but also ingenious. You might suddenly get an *aha* moment that can help your career and ambition. If you can add some humor and wit to whatever you do, it will take you far.

Uranus favors technology, innovation, and science. Maybe you can think of a great new application or an e-commerce business idea. It is also a good time to redo your website, give your Facebook page a face lift, and connect to social media. You will find yourself joining new virtual communities or joining new social media platforms. Make sure you are open to the new, exciting, and embrace the limitless possibility Uranus will present.

Your Hebrew Letter and Tarot Card:

Since 2020 is the year of 22, below is the Major Arcana card associated with your sign as well as the Hebrew letter. You can use the letter and place it inside the diamond in your meditation. The letter can also be used like a talisman to help you connect to your archetype. You will notice that in many cases, the letter's shape resembles its meaning. In my book *Cosmic Navigator*, you can find more information about the connection between the Hebrew letters and the zodiac signs.

Tarot: STRENGTH

Hebrew letter: Tet

The letter means "coiled serpent." It is believed that the Kundalini (coiled serpent) is metaphysically located in the tip of your spine and can rise when you are spiritually ready. Leo rules the spine and rules spirituality. Tet also means "good," and "kindness," reflecting Leo's generosity.

Summary:

2020 is an intense year that is filled with dramatic changes in your work and career. It is a year where you are asked to practice letting go and surrender as well as focus on your health. This year teaches you how to serve your body, your mission, and humanity.

VIRGO

New Karmic Cycle:
Love, Children, Creativity

2020 is a very interesting year. Leo is forced to learn to serve, while Virgo, the fixer and server, is asked to learn how to have fun, enjoy life, and well, be served. Indeed, it is during Saturnalia, the Roman celebration of Saturn, when roles were reversed and the social order upturned. The conjunction of Saturn, Pluto, and Jupiter fall in your house of children, love, happiness, and creativity. You are forced to change your way of looking at love and creativity. You can become a Mary Poppins, a person who serves childlike people or projects with a happy-go-lucky and magical approach. This year is the final semester of your happiness education before Saturn will move back into your house of work in 2021 and 2022. Saturn's transit in the house of work will help you infuse your workspace with the happiness and creativity that you have found in 2020. The last time you had Saturn in the house of happiness and love was between 1988 and early 1990.

You can go back to those years to see what lessons you learned about fun, creativity, children, and love. In 2020, you are asked to exercise openness of heart and the ability to see the world through a "child's mind." Your job is to be the kid, not the governess or the monk. You are practicing love, not your usual Virgo chastity. However, Pluto and Saturn can be a bit harsh in the way they teach these lessons and, since the conjunction falls in your house of children, there could be issues or the need to take responsibilities with your children or grandchildren. In addition, deep buried childhood memories might surface in order to be healed. But do not be discouraged because Jupiter, the planet of expansion and luck, is also moving into your house of love, creating an opportunity for you to open your heart and maybe even fall in love, if not with a person then with a hobby, a new passion, or a physical activity.

Between March and July, Saturn will move into your house of work, service, and health, and you will get a glimpse of the lessons that you need to learn in 2021 and 2022. There could be some changes in your work, health, and diet. So preventive medicine from the beginning of the year is recommended.

The eclipses this year continue their journey in your house of community and friends. Since the end of 2018, your job has been to be selective with your friends and find like-minded friends and colleagues.

From June this year, the eclipses shift into Gemini and Sagittarius, which are square to your sign. This means that until the end of 2021, you will be pushed and pulled between career and home and have to make some tough decisions regarding your professional and personal life.

Venus' long journey in Gemini, which is square to Virgo, can be a bit harsh between April and July. Watch your relationships, especially in your career and with your father and/or superiors. However, Venus is the goddess of love and she can bring new passions and interests which can translate as a boost in your income. Try to implement more creativity, art, and collaboration in your career at that time.

Uranus is in your house of travel and education which can manifest as an unexpected journey or a meeting with a foreigner or someone from a different race or religion that can help in your awakening. In addition, any form of technological studies or education can come unexpectedly. Be open!

The last six months of the year will be very interesting, since Mars, the energy of passion and sexuality, is moving into your house of sexuality, so love and sexuality are the highlights this year.

From July to December, Mars can help you find passion, create more intimacy in your life, and help let go of things you don't need. After all, Mars will transit in your house of death and transformation. Let the magic take hold!

The Six Eclipses
Your Emotional Landscape

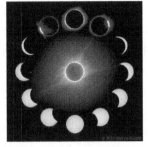

In Part I, I shared the meaning behind the eclipses as well as their Sabian symbols and paths. To make it easier, I have included some of that information below, as well as the way the eclipses manifest in your sign. The eclipses this year are a mixed bag for you. As you will see below, the eclipses that fall in Cancer and Capricorn are easier to handle. However, those that fall in Sagittarius and Gemini can be more challenging, since these signs form a square to your Sun, forcing you into actions you might not be comfortable with.

Jan 10 / 11: Penumbral Lunar eclipse in Cancer. Sabian symbol: Prima donna singing. Eclipse path: Europe, Asia, Australia, Africa, most of North America, east part of South America. Pacific, Atlantic, and Indian Oceans. To understand the story of this eclipse, let's return to the movie analogy. The first act of your story took place during the eclipses in July, 2019.

This January 10, 2020 eclipse is the second act of your film. The third and final act will be shot on the eclipse of July 5, 2020. Pay attention to synchronicities or anything out of the ordinary and try to link the events of the eclipses to a narrative. The eclipses fall in your house of friends, community, and corporations. However, the Full Moon creates an opposition between your children and your company, your love and your duty to work, your friends and your happiness. Situations might force you to split your time or choose between these oppositions. Try to integrate both, instead of choosing one over another.

June 5 / 6: Penumbral Lunar eclipse in Sagittarius. Sabian symbol: Seagulls watching a ship. Eclipse path: Europe, most of Asia, Australia, Africa, south / east South America, Pacific, Atlantic, Indian Oceans. This eclipse is the first of the new Gemini-Sagittarius axial eclipses. Truth versus lies, authentic against fake. This eclipse is a shift of focus and energy. The Moon and Sun are in opposition and they pull and push you between the houses of career and home. The last time you experienced these oppositions was in late 2001 and 2002. You might feel emotional and reactive, so try to focus on breathing, hiking, cardio, cycling, or swimming. **June 21: Solar Annular Solstice eclipse in Cancer.** Sabian symbol: A sailor ready to hoist a new flag to replace an old one. Eclipse path: south / east Europe, most of Asia, north Australia, most of Africa, Pacific, and Indian Oceans. In addition, this eclipse takes place during a retrograde bonanza: Mercury, Venus, Pluto, Saturn, Pallas, and Jupiter are all in retrograde motion. This means their expression is more internal and it will feel like you are a passenger in a car driven by a very bad driver.

Take extra care in how you relate to and communicate with lovers, friends, and authority figures. This Solar eclipse is introducing you to a new friend, a new community, or a new position in your organization. The eclipse can be an opportunity to meet new like-minded people. It can also help you manifest a dream or a wish — choose wisely.

July 4 / 5: Penumbral Lunar eclipse in Capricorn. Sabian symbol: An ancient bas-relief carved in granite. Eclipse path: south/west Europe, most of Africa, North America, South America, Pacific, Atlantic, and Indian Oceans. This eclipse is the mirror image of the Lunar eclipse of January 10 and therefore is the climax of whatever you started in July 2019. Mercury is retrograde during this eclipse, so we are still in danger of miscommunication and regretting our actions and / or choices. This eclipse is located in your house of children and community and these two areas of your life could come to the foreground. There could also be some issues in your love life and some challenges with your general sense of happiness and wellbeing.

Nov 29 / 30: Penumbral Lunar eclipse in Gemini. Sabian symbol: Quiver filled with arrows. Eclipse path: Europe, most of Asia, Australia, North America, South America, Pacific, and Atlantic Oceans. The eclipse continues the exploration of what is true and what is false. It is a time to change the way we learn and teach. Once again, there is an opposition between career and family, but since the North Node is in the house of career, make sure you do not sacrifice your true calling and career to pressures from family. Try not to be sucked into family drama.

Dec 14: Total Solar eclipse in Sagittarius. Sabian symbol: Blue bird standing at the door of the house. Eclipse path: South Africa, South America, Pacific, Atlantic, and Indian Oceans. This is a powerful eclipse that begins a new journey in education, travel, and publishing. You might encounter an inspiring mentor or become one for someone else. This is a good time for buying a new home, moving to a new place, or renovations.

Mercury Retrograde - *The Trickster*

Mercury is the trickster. Even when he is cruising direct through the heavens, he likes to pull practical jokes. I always thought that this was his compensation for delivering messages. When Mercury is retrograde, his tricks and ruses go to the next level. Of course, Mercury does not really retrograde, but from an earthly vantage point, Mercury looks as if he is going backwards three or four times a year for about three weeks.

Mercury, the messenger of the gods and goddesses, represents the archetype of communication, connections, computers, emails, texts, messages, directions, information, data, cables, Wi-Fi, the nervous system, and breathing. During Mercury retrograde, all these aspects of life are reversed, malfunctioning. Error messages, delays, accidents, mishaps, misspelling, and glitches plague the earth.

During Mercury retrograde, it is not recommended to start new long-term projects, sign documents, make

large purchases, get married, start marketing campaigns, publish, inaugurate locations or homes, or release new products. Communications of all sorts are slower and more challenging. Computers crash; stock markets turn volatile; flights are delayed; traffic is worse than usual; accidents occur more often; and Murphy's Law takes hold of all aspects of our lives. If you need to fly during Mercury retrograde, make sure you do your online check-in and give yourself enough time to reach the airport. Try to avoid overscheduling yourself or being overly critical and demanding. Also, pay attention to your diet and food intake.

If you must start a new project, be as mindful as you can. Pay attention to small details and read in-between the lines if you must sign a document. Rewrite your emails; edit your texts; and think before you speak or post. In fact, it is better if you spend more time listening than talking. Life does not come to a halt during Mercury retrograde. You can still achieve a great deal. It is like going on a vacation in Sweden in the winter: It can still be fun, just make sure you take a coat. However, Mercury retrograde is a great time to edit, redo, reexamine yourself and your path, revisit old projects, and find lost objects. Try to focus on activities that have the prefix *re* – reevaluate, reedit, redo, reexamine, reconnect, regenerate, revisit, re-imagine, etc.

Mercury is a liminal god and also a shadow-walker, a psychopomp, and a wizard (Hermetic studies are named after his Greek name). Jung identified him as the god of synchronicities, and it is true that during Mercury retrograde there are far more synchronicities and meaningful coincidences. Yes, you might have made it to the wrong place for your meeting, but there you bump into someone you have been unable to find for ages. Yes, you might have made it to the wrong place for your meeting, but there you might bump into someone you were unable to track for ages. And yes, you might arrive at the appointment at 9 AM instead of 9 PM, but because of that "mistake," you may have avoided a terrible accident.

Mercury is your ruler. He is the planet that gives you high intelligence, ability to pay attention to small details, and the sharp analytical gifts of your sign. When he is retrograde, perfect is disguised as imperfect and your analytical prowess is somewhat wrong or off-target. In other words, instead of cutting to the chase, you might be cutting your own fingers.

1st Retro: February 16 – March 10. From Feb 16 to March 4, Mercury retrogrades in Pisces and falls in your house of relationships and partnerships. Pisces is your opposite sign and that means Mercury is opposite to your Sun: either you will talk too much or too little.

There could be some issues with your partner in life or in work. From March 4 to March 10, Mercury is retrograde in Aquarius, which is your house of work, service, and health, the aspects of life that Virgo rules. There could be miscommunication with coworkers, employees, as well as issues with your health.

2nd Retro: June 18 – July 12. Mercury retrogrades in Cancer. Be careful with this one, since it takes place during the powerful eclipse on June 21st. Mercury is pulling his tricks in your house of friends and organizations. There could be miscommunications and misunderstanding within your company or with friends. Or, maybe a long-lost friend returns to your circle.

3rd Retro: Oct 13 – Nov 3. Mercury is retrograde in Scorpio between October 13 and October 28, when Mars is also retrograde. This double retro motion also happened in July and August 2018. You can go back and see what happened then and maybe avoid similar mistakes. This retrograde falls in your house of communications, writing, and contracts. This can be an especially difficult retrograde, so be careful with what you say or write. From October 28 to November 3 Mercury will be retrograde in Libra, your house of money, talents, and self-worth. Be mindful of pointless expenses.

Venus
Love, Pleasure, Art and Finance

Everyone loves Venus. Actually, what I just wrote, to an ancient Greek, would sound like a redundancy, since Venus embodies love and who does not love *love*?
But this year, it will be harder to love *love*, since Venus will be retrograding in Gemini between May 13 to June 25. She will be riding the Dragon, North Node, like an angry Khaleesi, who was just rejected by her John Snow. Venus goes retrograde once in 18 months for 40 days and 40 nights. It is a time we should dedicate to reevaluating our relationships, what we attract and what we are attracted to, how we relate to others, what talents we use to make money, as well as our core values and creeds. Some of us will have to confront insecurities and lower self-esteem during the retrograde. Many people change their attitudes, ideals, ethics, public image, dress code, and philosophies.
It is a good time to get out of contracts that are not good for you. Venus retrograde is a time when people are more blunt, combative, and lack diplomacy. You will also see a great deal of awkwardness on the world stage between diplomats as well as the court system.

When Venus is retrograde, it is not recommended to get engaged or married, form business partnerships, buy art, make investments, start lawsuits, or spend money. If you are planning a cosmetic operation or an IVF, better wait for Venus to forget about her rejection and land her dragon safely on greener pastures.

Venus retrograde in Gemini specifically deals with how we communicate with our significant others, as well as relationships with business partners, siblings, and relatives. During Venus' long journey in Gemini (April 3 to August 7), we have the opportunity to connect beauty, art and finance with communication, technology, and business. Letters merge with notes, numbers with colors. Your art can be communicative and your communication artistic.

The retrograde can bring back money owed to you and reconnect you with a talent or a project you have neglected in the past. You might also reconnect to a close friend from school.

Venus will be retrograding in your house of career. Be extra aware of your relationships with people you interact with in your career, especially bosses.

You will be judged not by your productivity and efficiency, but rather by your social skills. It is time to be a diplomat. However, since Venus is in your house of career between April and early August, you will find yourself being more creative and artistic in your vocation. These few months can also bring an interesting person into your life through your career. Open your eyes, mind, and heart.

From October 2 to October 28, Venus is in your sign. You feel attractive, desired, and lucky. You channel the qualities of beauty, diplomacy, and tact. You appear sympathetic, kind, and might even feel more flirtatious. Be careful not to overdo it and fall into vanity or largesse.

Mars
Assertion, Passion, Leadership

Mars is the engine of the zodiac. He is hot, driven, passionate, aggressive, explosive, and impulsive. He was named "Father of Rome" and he might have had his origins as a god of vegetation. Mars is still associated with spring and seeds. Even in Genesis 1:12, we find a trace of the connection between Mars and vegetation. On the third day of creation, that is, on "Martes" (day of Mars), God created vegetation and seeds. At least there is something on which monotheists and pagan agree. This year, Mars will be traveling from June 28 until the end of the year in Aries, even though he usually spends just a few weeks in a sign. Mars, the god of war, is the ruler of Aries, the sign of warfare. This does not necessarily mean war is upon us, but it does indicate there will be a great deal of strife, discord, and conflict. Astrology, like anything else in life is relative, so you might feel more belligerent than your usual self. Call it an Incredible-Hulk aspect: things, people, situations will drive us MADDDDDD!

This year, Mars will be retrograde in Aries between September 9 to November 14. When Mars is retrograde it is not a very auspicious time to start big projects with large investments. It is not a good time for surgery and medical procedures; neither is it recommended to start an intimate or sexual relationship. Avoid buying big machinery, making large investments, or starting wars or lawsuits. It is a more dangerous time, since wars, conflicts, explosions, and terror seem to follow Mars. After all, Mars' moons are called Phobos (fear) and Deimos (terror). If you need to fight, let the opponent fire the first bullet. Whoever starts a war with Mars retrograde, loses.

The Brexit referendum took place during Mars retrograde in Aquarius, the sign of government and community. And what happened right after? Oops, regret. What have we done? That is a typical Mars retrograde reaction. Another infamous example is the non-aggression treaty signed by Nazi Germany and the Soviets before WWII (Molotov-Ribbentrop). It was also a Mars retrograde station, and, obviously the treaty did not last long. Watch out for what agreements or treaties you sign, what you agree to, what you promise to do, what you fight for, and what you are willing to do to satiate your passions. Mars retrograde is a good time to review your past strategies, rethink your battles and wars, change direction in leadership, and admit that you were wrong.

Take extra care between October 13 and November 4, since both Mars and Mercury are retrograde. Miscommunications and misunderstandings can easily flare into full-fledged wars.

Below is a list of Mars transits through the signs that can help you determine where to focus your energy. However, remember that even the best fighters need a general. Make sure you pace yourself and control your inner warrior.

January 3 to February 16 – Mars in Sagittarius: This Mars transit gives you a good start to the year with energy and passion for travel, study, and authenticity. Mars is in your house of home and family and, while he can bring you energy to fix your home, renovate, or even move, he can also manifest as discord and fights with family members.

February 16 to March 30 – Mars in Capricorn: Mars, through the filter of Capricorn, exhibits his best qualities. He is the trained martial artist, fighting only when it is needed and he can easily win. However, be aware that Mercury retrograde might slow things down. Mars is plowing through your house of children, love, and happiness. Mars wants you to be active, entertaining, and fun. Spend time outdoors and initiate recreational activities. It is a good time for a creative project or a new hobby.

March 30 to May 13 – Mars in Aquarius: This is a good time to fight for your ideals, for your group and company or come to the rescue of a friend in need. However, it can also create conflict with certain friends or people in your company. Mars is in your house of diet, health, and work. It is a good time for Virgo, as these aspects of life are especially important to you. This is a time to start a new exercise routine, initiate a new project in work, fight for a promotion, or explore new leadership roles in your workplace. Don't wait for things to happen. Make them manifest! Watch your health, head injuries as well as accidents. Mars in this house can manifest as conflicts with employees and coworkers.

May 13 to June 28 – Mars in Pisces: With this transit of Mars, you have to make sure you are getting enough sleep and rest. Give time for your immune system to recover. It is a good time for interval fasting as well as for meditation and yoga. Two powerful eclipses, as well as Venus retrograde are taking place and it can be intense out there. It is a good time for physical activities near or in water such as swimming, surfing, rowing, hiking / running / cycling by a body of water. Mars is in your house of relationships and partnership — in these six weeks there may be increased conflict, or just more energy with your significant others. Be careful of enemies and antagonists and choose your battles wisely. Any sport or physical activity done in partnership is favored.

June 29 – End of the Year – Mars in Aries: Mars likes to be home in Aries, the sign of his rulership. The king is back in his palace. However, it can get hot and aggressive. Mars in Aries can be domineering. So back off and don't be overly cocky or too pushy. Lead through example and not fear or intimidation. It is a good time to explore, do things you never did, ask for a raise, and put your foot down. However, remember that between

September 9 and November 14, Mars is retrograde. Some delays and a pushback from life will take place. It might feel as if you are hitting the brakes after going 100 mph. This aspect of Mars can help connect you to your passion and sexuality as well as to your life force. Joint artistic and financial affairs might force you to take a leadership role. There could be a call to action concerning working with other people's talent and money. Mars will also give you the will and power to let go of things that hold you back.

Uranus - *Unpredictability, Originality, and a Touch of Chaos*

In March 2019, Uranus made his final move into Taurus, which is located in your house of travel and education, and will stay there until 2026. This transit of Uranus can manifest as a sudden journey abroad, an unexpected opportunity to teach or learn, and a deep need to explore new intellectual horizons. This is a good aspect for publishing work in mass media, online, blogging, social media, TV, or magazines, especially if the subject matter can be wrapped with humor. If you are a teacher, you will find yourself being funnier and, if you are a student, an original mad-professor style teacher or mentor might come into your life. After all, Uranus is called "the Joker" or "the Fool".

Uranus favors technology, innovation, and science. Maybe you can think of a great new application or an e-commerce business idea. It is also a good time to redo your website, give your Facebook page a face lift, and connect to social media. You will find yourself joining new virtual communities or joining new social media platforms, especially if they are from a different culture or relate to information and education.

Your Hebrew Letter and Tarot Card:

Since 2020 is the year of 22, below is the Major Arcana card associated with your sign as well as the Hebrew letter. You can use the letter and place it inside the diamond in your meditation. The letter can also be used like a talisman to help you connect to your archetype. You will notice that in many cases, the letter's shape resembles its meaning. In my book *Cosmic Navigator*, you can find more information about the connection between the Hebrew letters and the zodiac signs.

Tarot: THE HERMIT

Hebrew letter: Yod

The hand of God. It is the smallest letter of the alphabet but also the one that is used to draw all the rest. Yod is the letter that, true to its Virgo association, serves all the rest of the alphabet. It is like a pixel.

Summary:

2020 is an intense year that will force you to look into your love, happiness, and focus on children. Since Mars will spend six months in your house of passion and intimacy, he will propel you to look deeper into your sexuality. Choose your friends and groups wisely this year and for all of our sakes, learn how to have fun!

LIBRA

New Karmic Cycle:
Home and Family

2020 is an emotional year. The next twelve months ask you to emote, to experience life through your heart, and raise you EQ to support your typically high IQ. Since the end of 2017, you have been asking yourself questions such as: where do I want to live? Where is my abode? Where do I feel safe? Who do I want to live with? The last time you were dealing with these questions was 1989 – 1991 and now, with Jupiter entering your house of home, he will bring some answers and opportunities for you to finally settle down. However, in January, the powerful conjunction of Pluto and Saturn creates a major shift in your life. It is a tectonic change with everything that has to do with family, real estate, and land. Some of you will get pregnant, buy a new property, move homes, or face some responsibilities with your family of origin or new family. However, from mid-March to the end of June, Saturn moves into Aquarius which will be easier for you because Saturn in Capricorn is square to your sign. Saturn in Aquarius focuses you on love, children, and creativity. In 2021 and 2022, Saturn will return to Aquarius and, in those years, you will experience a renewal of interest in children, happiness, and love. Since the end of 2018, and through June 2020, the eclipses are squaring your sign which made things speed up in your career, as well as home and family. From June this year, the eclipses are moving into Gemini, a fellow Air-Bender, and it will literally feel like you can breathe again. The eclipses from June 2020 until the end of 2021 take place in your house of travel and higher education. These areas of your life will feel like they are going faster and coming to a resolution.

In the last six months of 2020, Mars moves in your house of relationships and marriage. Mars' transit in that house can manifest as arguments or discord with partners in life or in work, especially September through early November when Mars is retrograde. Mars can also bring energy, passion, and action into your relationships. However, be extra careful with antagonists and enemies, people's jealousy, and lawsuits. You are the sign of peace, but Mars can stir things up and test your famously strong ability to compromise.

In 2019, Uranus, the Joker, entered your house of sexuality and passion. Uranus can awaken a new passion in life, helping you attract new opportunities, especially when working with other people's talents and money. But Uranus would like you to also experiment with letting go, and "killing" things in your life that hold you back. There could be an unexpected change and sudden death around you but, most of the time, this aspect indicates an abrupt change in routine and a new path which unveils itself and helps you tap into your hidden powers.

The Six Eclipses
Your Emotional Landscape

In Part I, I shared the meaning behind the eclipses and their Sabian symbols and paths. To make it easier, I have included some of that information below, as well as the way the eclipses manifest in your sign.

The eclipses this year are a mixed bag for you. As you will see below, those that fall in Cancer and Capricorn are creating a square with your sign. But, from June, the Dragon ascends to fly in a fellow air sign, Gemini which will make the eclipses easier to handle, at least until the end of 2021.

Jan 10 / 11: Penumbral Lunar eclipse in Cancer. Sabian symbol: Prima donna singing. Eclipse path: Europe, Asia, Australia, Africa, most of North America, east part of South America, Pacific, Atlantic, and Indian Oceans. To understand the story of this eclipse, let's return to the movie analogy. The first act of your story took place during the eclipses in July 2019. The eclipse of January 10, 2020 is the second act of your film. The third and final act is performed on the eclipse of July 5, 2020. Pay attention to synchronicities or anything out of the ordinary taking place during these dates and try to link the events of the eclipses to a narrative. The eclipses fall in your house of career and father figures which shows a feeling of extra responsibilities in your career and the need to prove yourself to your superiors or bosses. It can be a bit emotional at work and little things can trigger a big response. The eclipse can help you let go of your family's expectations and focus more on your professional life.

June 5 / 6: Penumbral Lunar eclipse in Sagittarius.
Sabian symbol: Seagulls watching a ship. Eclipse path: Europe, most of Asia, Australia, Africa, south / east South America, Pacific, Atlantic, and Indian Oceans. This eclipse is the first of the new Gemini-Sagittarius axial eclipses. Truth versus lies, authentic against fake. This eclipse is a shift of focus and energy. The North Node is moving into Gemini and you can cash in on some good karma. This eclipse asks you to focus on travel and education, being authentic, as well as staying away from lies and secrets.

June 21: Solar Annular Solstice eclipse in Cancer.
Sabian symbol: A sailor ready to hoist a new flag to replace an old one. Eclipse path: South / east Europe, most of Asia, North Australia, most of Africa, Pacific, and Indian Oceans. In addition, this eclipse takes place during a retrograde bonanza: Mercury, Venus, Pluto, Saturn, Pallas, and Jupiter are all in retrograde motion. This means their expression is more internal and it will feel like you are a passenger in a car driven by a very bad driver. Take extra care in how you relate to, and

communicate with lovers, friends, and authority figures. This Solar eclipse can bring about a swift new beginning in your career, a new project, or a new career path. The key to success is to "feel it," that is, to trust your gut feelings and intuition instead of your rationalizing mind.

July 4 / 5: Penumbral Lunar eclipse in Capricorn. Sabian symbol: An ancient bas-relief carved in granite. Eclipse path: south / west Europe, most of Africa, North America, South America, Pacific, Atlantic, and Indian Oceans. This eclipse is the mirror image of the Lunar eclipse of January 10 and therefore is the climax of whatever started in July 2019. Mercury is retrograde during this eclipse, therefore, we are still in danger of miscommunication and regretting our actions and / or choices. This last eclipse can be a bit emotional, especially with family members. Remember not to be distracted by home and family and stay true to your career.

Nov 29 / 30: Penumbral Lunar eclipse in Gemini. Sabian symbol: Quiver filled with arrows. Eclipse path: Europe, most of Asia, Australia, North America, South America, Pacific and Atlantic Oceans. The eclipse continues the exploration of what is true and what is false. It is a time to change the way we learn and teach. This eclipse can create some drama with in-laws, and if you are traveling abroad, take extra care. The eclipse forces you to walk the talk and be very honest with yourself or others. Some of your values might be tested.

Dec 14: Total Solar eclipse in Sagittarius. Sabian symbol: Blue bird standing at the door of the house. Eclipse path: South Africa, South America, Pacific, Atlantic, and Indian Oceans. This is a powerful eclipse that begins a new journey in education, travel, and publishing. You might encounter an inspiring mentor or become one for someone else. This eclipse can help kick start a new business, sign a new contract, or start a writing project.

Mercury Retrograde - *The Trickster*

Mercury is the trickster. Even when he is cruising direct through the heavens, he likes to pull practical jokes. I always thought that this was his compensation for delivering messages. When Mercury is retrograde, his tricks and ruses go to the next level. Of course, Mercury does not really retrograde, but from an earthly vantage point, Mercury does look as if he is going backwards three or four times a year for about three weeks. Mercury, the messenger of the gods and goddesses, represents the archetype of communication, connections, computers, emails, texts, messages, directions, information, data, cables, Wi-Fi, the nervous system, and breathing. During Mercury retrograde, all these aspects of life are reversed, malfunctioning. Error messages, delays, accidents, mishaps, misspelling, and glitches plague the earth.

During Mercury retrograde, it is not recommended to start new long-term projects, sign documents, make large purchases, get married, start marketing campaigns, publish, inaugurate locations or homes, or release new products. Communications of all sorts are slower and more challenging. Computers crash; stock markets turn volatile; flights are delayed; traffic is worse than usual; accidents occur more often; and Murphy's Law takes hold of all aspects of our lives. If you need to fly during Mercury retrograde, make sure you do your online check-in and allow enough time to reach the airport. Try to avoid overscheduling yourself or being overly critical and demanding. Also pay attention to your diet and food intake.

If you must start a new project, be as mindful as you can. Pay attention to small details and read in-between the lines if you must sign a document. Rewrite your emails; edit your texts; and think before you speak or post. In fact, it is better if you spend more time listening than talking. Life does not come to a halt during Mercury retrograde. You can still achieve a great deal. . It is like going on a vacation in Sweden in the winter: It can still be fun, just make sure you take a coat. However, Mercury retrograde is a great time to edit, redo, reexamine yourself and your path, revisit old projects, and find lost objects. Try to focus on activities that have the prefix *re* – reevaluate, reedit, redo, reexamine, reconnect, regenerate, revisit, re-imagine, etc.

Mercury is a liminal god and also a shadow-walker, a psychopomp, and a wizard (Hermetic studies are named after his Greek name). Jung identified him as the god of synchronicities, and it is true that during Mercury retrograde there are far more synchronicities and meaningful coincidences. Yes, you might have made it to the wrong place for your meeting, but there you bump into someone you have been unable to track for ages. And yes, you might arrive to the appointment at 9 AM instead of 9 PM, but because of that "mistake," you avoided a terrible accident.

As a Libra, you are fond of Mercury and his tricks. He is fun and intelligent. Even your ruler, Venus, once made love to Mercury and their child was the hermaphrodite, Hermaphroditus (a combination of the Greek names for Venus and Mercury). However, Mercury retrograding in water signs can be a bit more confusing for you. Pay attention to the Mercury retrograde in your sign between October 28 to November 3. These ten days can be extra problematic but a good time for editing or reconnecting to previously neglected projects or people.

1st Retro: February 16 – March 10. From Feb 16 to March 4 Mercury is retrograde in Pisces. Since Mercury retrogrades in your house of work and health, be extra careful with your immune system. There could be misunderstanding with coworkers and employees. Stick to your routine and diet but be flexible.

From March 4 to March 10, Mercury is retrograde in Aquarius, which is your house of love, children, and creativity. It is a good time to revisit old, unfinished, creative projects. Old flames might return to your life. Children can cause a bit of a headache.

2nd Retro: June 18 – July 12. Mercury retrogrades in Cancer. Be careful with this one, since it takes place during the powerful eclipse on June 21st. Mercury is pulling his tricks in your house of career, so be mindful of how you talk, text, or email your superiors or people in your career.

3rd Retro: Oct 13 – Nov 3. Mercury is retrograde in Scorpio between October 13 and October 28, when Mars is also retrograde. This retrograde takes place right when Mars is also retrograde. This double retro motion also happened in July and August 2018. You can go back to that time and see what happened and maybe avoid similar mistakes. This retrograde falls in your house of money and self-worth and may manifest as mood and energy swings or some issues with self-worth. Be extra careful with pointless expenses. From October 28 to November 3 Mercury will be retrograde in Libra, which falls in your sign, so be careful with your health. People in general might have the wrong impression of you, so focus on explaining yourself clearly.

Venus
Love, Pleasure, Art and Finance

Everyone loves Venus, your ruler. Actually, what I just wrote, to an ancient Greek, would sound like a redundancy, since Venus embodies love and who does not love *love*?

But this year, it will be harder to love love, since Venus will be retrograding in Gemini between May 13 to June 25. She will be riding the Dragon, North Node, like an angry Khaleesi, who was just rejected by her John Snow. Venus goes retrograde once in 18 months for 40 days and 40 nights. It is a time we should dedicate to reevaluating our relationships, what we attract and what we are attracted to, how we relate to others, what talents we use to make money, as well as our core values and creeds. Some of us will have to confront insecurities and lower self-esteem during the retrograde.

Many people change their attitudes, ideals, ethics, public image, dress code, and philosophies. It is a good time to get out of contracts that are not good for you. Venus retrograde is a time when people are more blunt, combative, and lack diplomacy. You will also see a great deal of awkwardness on the world stage between diplomats as well as in the court system.

When Venus is retrograde, it is not recommended to get engaged or married, form business partnerships, buy art, make investments, start lawsuits, or spend money. If you are planning a cosmetic operation or an IVF, better wait for Venus to forget about her rejection and land her dragon safely on greener pastures.

Venus retrograde in Gemini specifically deals with how we communicate with our significant others, as well as relationships with business partners, siblings, and relatives. During Venus' long journey in Gemini (April 3 to August 7), we have the opportunity to connect beauty, art and finance with communication, technology, and business. Letters merge with notes, numbers with colors. Your art can be communicative and your communication artistic.

The retrograde can bring back money owed to you and reconnect you with a talent or a project you have neglected in the past. You might also reconnect to a close friend from school.

Venus, your planet, will be retrograding in your house of higher-education, truth, travel, and philosophy. This is a great time to reevaluate your values, philosophies, and creeds. It is as if you are going through a constitutional crisis and need to change your mission statement. However, since Venus will be in your house of travel and education (April – early August) for such a long time this year, she can color your education and intellectual interest with art, design, and justice. It is not a bad time to travel to a new place. You might find that location familiar and maybe even fall in love with someone while traveling.

From October 28 to November 21, Venus is in your sign. You feel attractive, desired, and lucky. You channel the qualities of beauty, diplomacy, and tact. You appear sympathetic, kind, and might even feel more flirtatious. Be careful not to overdo it and fall into vanity and largesse.

Mars
Assertion, Passion, Leadership

Mars is the engine of the zodiac. He is hot, driven, passionate, aggressive, explosive, and impulsive. The Romans saw him as their father and some scholars trace his mythological origins as a god of vegetation. Mars is still associated with spring and seeds. Even in Genesis 1:12, we find a hint of the connection between Mars and vegetation. On the third day of creation, that is on "Martes" (day of Mars), God created vegetation and seeds: "Let the earth burst forth with every sort of grass and seed-bearing plant, and fruit trees with seeds inside the fruit, so that these seeds will produce the kinds of plants and fruits they came from." And so it was, and God was pleased.

Between June 28 and the end of the year, Mars will be traveling in Aries. This is abnormal as Mars usually spends about six weeks, not six months, in a sign. Mars, the god of war, is the ruler of Aries, the sign of warfare.

Yes, this can raise the probability of armed conflict, cyber-attacks, and other displays of aggression. This transit indicates there will be a great deal of strife, discord, and conflict. Astrology, like anything else in life is relative, so you might feel more belligerent than your usual self. Call it an Incredible-Hulk aspect: things, people, and situations will drive you MADDDDDD! This year, Mars will be retrograde in Aries between September 9 and November 14. When Mars is retrograde, it is not a very auspicious time to start big projects with large investments. It is not a good time for surgery and medical procedures unless urgent. Neither is it recommended to start an intimate or sexual relationship. Avoid buying big machinery, making large investments, or starting wars or lawsuits. It is a more dangerous time, since wars, conflicts, explosions, and terror seem to follow Mars. After all, Mars' moons are called Phobos (fear) and Deimos (terror). If you need to fight, let the opponent fire the first bullet. Whoever starts a war with Mars retrograde, loses.

The Brexit referendum took place during Mars retrograde in Aquarius, the sign of government and community. And what happened right after? Oops, regret. What have we done? That is a typical Mars retrograde reaction. Another infamous example is the non-aggression treaty signed by Nazi Germany and the Soviets before WWII (Molotov-Ribbentrop).

It was also a Mars retrograde station, and, obviously did not last long. Even though Mars retrograde is not the same as Mercury retrograde, avoid signing treaty or agreements that deal with action, wars, or campaigns. Be mindful of what you agree to do, what you promise to carry out, what you fight for, and what you are willing to do to satiate your passions. Mars retrograde is a good time to review your past strategies, rethink your battles and wars, change direction in leadership, and admit that you were wrong.

Take extra care between October 13 and November 4, since both Mars and Mercury are retrograde. Miscommunications and misunderstandings can easily flare into full-fledged wars.

Below is a list of Mars transits through the signs that can help you determine where to focus your energy. However, remember that even the best fighters need a general. Make sure you pace yourself and control your inner warrior.

January 3 to February 16 – Mars in Sagittarius: This Mars transit gives you a good start to the year with energy and passion for travel, study, and authenticity. Mars is traveling in your house of communication and relatives. He gives you a boost of energy in study, writing, and socializing, which is always great for a Libra. However, he can create some challenges or a need to work with relatives and siblings.

February 16 to March 30 – Mars in Capricorn: Mars through the filter of Capricorn exhibits his best qualities. He is the trained martial artist, fighting only when it is needed and he can easily win. However, be aware that Mercury retrograde might slow things down. Mars is in your house of home and family and, while he can bring you energy to fix your home, renovate, or even move, he can also manifest as discord and fights with family members.

March 30 to May 13 – Mars in Aquarius: This is a good time to fight for your ideals, for your group and company, and come to the rescue of a friend in need. However, it can also create conflict with certain friends or people in your company. Mars is plowing through your house of children, love, and happiness. Mars wants you to be active, entertaining, and fun. Spend time outdoors and initiate recreational activities. It is also a good time for a creative project or a new hobby.

May 13 to June 28 – Mars in Pisces: With this transit of Mars, you have to make sure you are getting enough sleep and rest. Give time for your immune system to recover. It is a good time for interval fasting as well as for meditation and yoga. Two powerful eclipses, as well as Venus retrograde, are taking place and it can be intense out there.

It is a good time for physical activities near or in water such as swimming, surfing, rowing, hiking / running / cycling by a body of water. Mars is in your house of diet, health, and work. This is a time to start a new exercise routine, initiate a new project in work, fight for a promotion, or explore new leadership roles in your workplace. Don't wait for things to happen. Make them happen! Watch your health, head injuries as well as accidents. Mars in this house can manifest as conflicts with employees and coworkers.

June 29 – End of the Year – Mars in Aries: Mars likes to be home in Aries, the sign of his rulership. The king is back in his palace. However, it can get hot and aggressive. Mars in Aries can be domineering. So back off and don't be overly cocky or too pushy. Lead through example and not fear or intimidation. It is a good time to explore, do things you never did, ask for a raise, and put your foot down. However, remember that between September 9 and November 14, Mars is retrograde. Some delays and a pushback from life will take place. It might feel as if you are hitting the brakes after going 100 mph. Mars' six month journey in house of relationships and partnership suggests that there could be a great deal of conflict, or just increased energy, with your significant others. Be careful of enemies and antagonists and choose your battles wisely. Any sport or physical activity done in partnership is favored.

Uranus - *Unpredictability, Originality, and a Touch of Chaos*

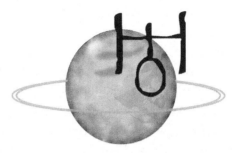

In March 2019, Uranus made his final move into Taurus, which is located in your house of sexuality, passion, magic, transformation, death, and resurrection. It does sound a bit morbid, and in some ways it is. Uranus is unpredictable. So if you expect it to be bad, it might actually be good. But seriously, Uranus shakes things up and can create sudden opportunities to dramatically change where you live, how you look, what you do, etc. Uranus has already been in that house for a year — it is not a new aspect. However, it is good to know that the Joker and Fool is in your house of transformation until 2026. For the next few years, you might need to work more with technology, science, communities, and even nonprofit organizations. The most important thing is to be open to new possibilities and embrace change.

Uranus can also create sudden changes in your passion and what you attract or are attracted to, not only sexually but also emotionally, intellectually, and even spiritually. There could be a sudden death but usually Uranus is not the grim reaper. Rather, he is the awakener. The sleeper must awaken!

Uranus favors technology, innovation, and science. Maybe you can think of a great new application or an e-commerce business idea. It is also a good time to redo your website, give your Facebook page a face lift, and connect to social media. You will find yourself joining new virtual communities or join new social media platforms, especially if they are from a different culture or relate to information and education.

Your Hebrew Letter and Tarot Card:

Since 2020 is the year of 22, below is the Major Arcana card associated with your sign as well as the Hebrew letter. You can use the letter and place it inside the diamond in your meditation. The letter can also be used like a talisman to help you connect to your archetype. You will notice that in many cases, the letter's shape resembles its meaning. In my book *Cosmic Navigator*, you can find more information about the connection between the Hebrew letters and the zodiac signs.

Tarot: JUSTICE

Hebrew letter: Lamed

ל

The letter means both "to learn" and "to teach." This is the secret of Libra – the perfect relationship is when you and your partner equality learn from and teach each other. The letter is located right in the middle of the alphabet, just like Libra is in the center of the zodiac, representing balance and harmony.

Summary:

2020 is an intense year that will force you to look into your dwelling, home, family, and emotional life. The year can help you tie up loose ends, especially in connection to childhood and familial issues. If you want to buy a property or get pregnant (physically or metaphysically), 2020 presents many opportunities for manifesting these things. The year asks you to be true to yourself and your beliefs and look deep into your passion and what you want to summon into your life.

SCORPIO

New Karmic Cycle:
The Power of the Word

The year 2020 continues your journey into the depth and mystery of the *Logos* – the power of the word. If there is a sign that is a vessel for the idea of magic, it is Scorpio, the sign of transformation and the occult. Of all magic spells, the most commonly cited is *abracadabra.* The word is in Aramaic (the root language of Semitic tongues, i.e., Hebrew and Arabic), which according to Jewish lore, is the language of angels. Abracadabra means "I will create as I speak." This relates to the ancient Greek idea of *Logos.* As the New Testament asserts (John 1:1), "In the beginning, there was the word and the word was God." The powerful conjunction of January 2020 initiates a cycle of 30 years in your house of communication and spells. You are learning first-hand, not always smoothly, how to take responsibility over your words, texts, emails, memos, or any other form of communication you deploy. This is not an easy lesson for you as a mute sign known for keeping secrets. You are the spy, the private investigator, the poker-faced, lips-sealed sign. Learning to communicate better does not reflect on how much more you speak or write but rather on the quality, timing, and meaning of your messages. In other words, Pluto, Saturn, Jupiter, as well as the South Node, are asking you to change, morph, and consolidate the message you want to deliver to humanity. Since Jupiter moves into your house of communication this year, he facilitates the flow of data and information as well as communication. Other areas in your life where there might be challenges or changes are with relatives, siblings, and neighbors. There might be a need to reach out or help your relatives, fix issues there, or help a neighbor. Saturn might also ask you to look into your contracts and renegotiate or altogether break some of your agreements. Again, the power of the word also means paying attention to the small print in your contacts.

This year is a good year to start a new businesses and dive into new deals, leads, or trade. Since the eclipses are taking place in your house of foreign cultures and higher education, some of the business opportunities could come from abroad or in connection to education, mass media, and / or publishing. Focus on media and communication and, in some way you will have to let go of the shroud of secrecy and expose, market, and promote yourself or your projects.

An interesting synchronicity is that the North Node moves into Gemini, the sign of communication in June. This aids your journey into the realm of the word, and falls in your house of magic, passion, and sexuality, which is your natural domain. This suggests that the right words at the right time can truly help you connect to your passions and intimacy.

From mid-March to early July, Saturn will momentarily move into Aquarius, and therefore into your house of home and family. There could be some difficulties or a need to shift focus to family members, parents, or real estate. This will be a precursor of things to come in 2021-2022 and is similar to what you experienced in 1991-1992.

Uranus is now in your house of relationships and marriage and will be there until 2026. Your partner in work or in life might be going through some unpredictable transitions. A new spark is entering your significant relationships. Embrace it and get ready for a roller coaster ride. If you don't have a partner, there will be sudden, unpredictable infusions of potential partners. Some of them are jokers and fools. Others are ingenious and a lot of them flaky. Choose your partner wisely. But regardless, it means that you need more freedom in your relationships in the next six years.

In the last six months of the year, Mars, your planet, will be traveling in your house of health, diet, and work. There will be a great urge to push and lead projects in work, and you will be called to a position of management or leadership. However, watch your health — especially injuries, inflammations, or accidents. There might be some challenges with co-workers and employees from September to mid-November, when Mars is retrograde.

This year take control of the power of the word and you can make magic happen: Thoughts can translate into words that can manifest as actions. Since the North Node will be in your house of other people's money and talent, you will find yourself directly helping people around you, or tapping into their inner resources.

The Six Eclipses
Your Emotional Landscape

In Part I, I shared the meaning behind the eclipses and their Sabian symbols and paths. To make it easier, I have included some of that information below, as well as the way the eclipses manifest in your sign.

The eclipses this year are a mixed bag for you. As you will see below, those that fall in Cancer (water sign) and Capricorn (earth sign) are harmonious with you, since you are a Water-Bender and can channel the changes of those eclipses more easily. But from June, the Dragon ascends to fly in Gemini, the sign that rules communication. As you saw, 2020 is the year where you are mastering communication. The Dragon in Gemini can help you or, better still, force you to focus on your words, marketing, and messages.

Jan 10 / 11: Penumbral Lunar eclipse in Cancer. Sabian symbol: Prima donna singing. Eclipse path: Europe, Asia, Australia, Africa, most of North America, east part of South America, Pacific, Atlantic, and Indian Oceans.

To understand the story of this eclipse, let's return to the movie analogy. The first act of your story took place during the eclipses of July 2019. This January 10, 2020, eclipse is the second act of your film. The third and final act will be shot on the eclipse of July 5, 2020. Pay attention to synchronicities or anything out of the ordinary and try to link the events of the eclipses to a narrative. The eclipses fall in your house of truth, philosophy, education, and travel. Sounds fun? However, this eclipse pits truth versus lies, your philosophies versus the need to promote and push your message. This is the time where your message for the next 30 years will be downloaded. Take time to formulate it.

June 5 / 6: Penumbral Lunar eclipse in Sagittarius.
Sabian symbol: Seagulls watching a ship. Eclipse path: Europe, most of Asia, Australia, Africa, south / east South America, Pacific, Atlantic, Indian Oceans. This eclipse is the first of the new Gemini-Sagittarius axial eclipses. This eclipse is a shift of focus and energy. The North Node is moving into Gemini and is forcing you to look into what moves your soul, what drives you, what your passion is. The next 18 months will help you let go and cut away things that hold you back, obstacles, or blocks in your life. There is much magic in the air during these eclipses.

June 21: Solar Annular Solstice eclipse in Cancer.
Sabian symbol: A sailor ready to hoist a new flag to replace an old one.

Eclipse path: south / east Europe, most of Asia, north Australia, most of Africa, Pacific, and Indian Oceans. In addition, this eclipse takes place during a retrograde bonanza: Mercury, Venus, Pluto, Saturn, Pallas, and Jupiter are all in retrograde motion. This means their expression is more internal and it will feel like you are a passenger in a car driven by a very bad driver. Take extra care in how you talk to and communicate with lovers, friends, and authority figures. This Solar eclipse is can bring about a swift new beginning in your connection to education and travel. There could be a new intellectual interest, a need to study a new language, or travel to a new country. This is a good eclipse to publish something or fix relationships with in-laws.

July 4 / 5: Penumbral Lunar eclipse in Capricorn. Sabian symbol: An ancient bas-relief carved in granite. Eclipse path: south / west Europe, most of Africa, North America, South America, Pacific, Atlantic, and Indian Oceans. This eclipse is the mirror image of the Lunar eclipse of January 10 and therefore is the climax of whatever started for you in July 2019. Mercury is retrograde during this eclipse, therefore, we are still in danger of miscommunication and regretting our actions and / or choices. Be extra careful with what you write, sign, or publish. This eclipse can be emotional and cause some friction with in-laws or foreigners.

Nov 29 / 30: Penumbral Lunar eclipse in Gemini. Sabian symbol: Quiver filled with arrows. Eclipse path: Europe, most of Asia, Australia, North America, South America,

Pacific, and Atlantic Oceans. The eclipse continues the exploration of what is true and what is false. It is a time to change the way we learn and teach. This eclipse pits your money versus your partner's money or perhaps your values versus your partner's.

Dec 14: Total Solar eclipse in Sagittarius. Sabian symbol: Blue bird standing at the door of the house. Eclipse path: South Africa, South America, Pacific, Atlantic and Indian Oceans. This is a powerful eclipse that begins a new journey in education, travel, and publishing. You might encounter an inspiring mentor or become one for someone else. This eclipse can bring about a boost in your income or some financial opportunity. It is a good time to travel to a country you have never been to before.

Mercury Retrograde - *The Trickster*

Mercury is the trickster. Even when he is cruising direct through the heavens, he likes to pull practical jokes. I always thought that this was his compensation for delivering messages. When Mercury is retrograde, his tricks and ruses go to the next level. Of course, Mercury does not really retrograde, but from an earthly vantage point, Mercury does look as if he is going backwards three or four times a year for about three weeks. Mercury, the messenger of the gods and goddesses, represents the archetype of communication, connections, computers, emails, texts, messages, directions, information, data, cables, Wi-Fi, the nervous system, and breathing. During Mercury retrograde, all these aspects of life are reversed, malfunctioning. Error messages, delays, accidents, mishaps, misspelling, and glitches plague the earth.

During Mercury retrograde, it is not recommended to start new long-term projects, sign documents, make

large purchases, get married, start marketing campaigns, publish, inaugurate locations or homes, or release new products. Communications of all sorts are slower and more challenging. Computers crash; stock markets turn volatile; flights are delayed; traffic is worse than usual; accidents occur more often; and Murphy's Law takes hold of all aspects of our lives. If you need to fly during Mercury retrograde, make sure you do your online check-in and allow more time to reach the airport. Try to avoid overscheduling yourself or being overly critical and demanding. Also pay attention to your diet and food intake.

If you must start a new project, be as mindful as you can. Pay attention to small details and read in-between the lines if you must sign a document. Rewrite your emails; edit your texts; and think before you speak or post. In fact, it is better if you spend more time listening than talking. Life does not come to a halt during Mercury retrograde. You can still achieve a great deal during his retrograde. It is like going on a vacation in Sweden in the winter: It can still be fun, just make sure you take a coat. However, Mercury retrograde is a great time to edit, redo, reexamine yourself and your path, revisit old projects, and find lost objects. Try to focus on activities that have the prefix *re* – reevaluate, reedit, redo, reexamine, reconnect, regenerate, revisit, re-imagine, etc. Mercury is a liminal god and also a shadow-walker, a psychopomp, and a wizard (Hermetic studies are named after his Greek name). Jung identified him as the god of synchronicities, and it is true that during Mercury retrograde there are far more synchronicities and meaningful coincidences. Yes, you might have made it to the wrong place for your meeting, but there you bump into someone you have been unable to track for ages. And yes, you might arrive at the appointment at 9 AM instead of 9 PM, but because of that "mistake," you may have avoided a terrible accident.

This year, Mercury being the ruler of communication and the messenger of the gods and goddesses is very important to you as your focus is on communication. When Mercury is retrograde it is a good time to reevaluate how you communicate. Be extra careful when Mercury retrogrades in your sign between October 14 - 28, especially if you are born during these dates.

1st Retro: February 16 – March 10. From Feb 16 to March 4 Mercury is retrograde in Pisces which is a fellow water sign. This makes it is a bit easier, but you can expect some challenges in communications with children or lovers. Old creative projects might return. From March 4 to March 10, Mercury is retrograde in Aquarius, which is your house of family and real estate. There could be some miscommunication with family mummers.

2nd Retro: June 18 – July 12. Mercury retrogrades in Cancer. Be careful with this one, since it takes place during the powerful eclipse on June 21st. Mercury is pulling his tricks in your house of travel and education. If you are a teacher or a student, it can be a bit more difficult to retain or deliver information.

3rd Retro: Oct 13 – Nov 3. Mercury is retrograde in Scorpio between October 13 and October 28, when Mars is also retrograde. This double retro motion also happened in July and August 2018. You can go back and see what happened then and maybe avoid similar mistakes. This retrograde falls in your sign and can manifest as challenges in health and your ability to present yourself in the proper way. From October 28 to November 3 Mercury will be retrograde in Libra, which falls in your house of letting go, surrender, and separation. There could be more access to memories from past lives, imagination, empathy, and an emotional openness and vulnerability.

Venus
Love, Pleasure, Art and Finance

Everyone loves Venus. Actually, what I just wrote, to an ancient Greek, would sound like a redundancy, since Venus embodies love and who does not love *love*?

But this year, it will be harder to love love, since Venus will be retrograding in Gemini between May 13 to June 25. She will be riding the Dragon, North Node, like an angry Khaleesi, who was just rejected by her John Snow. Venus goes retrograde once in 18 months for 40 days and 40 nights. It is a time we should dedicate to reevaluating our relationships, what we attract and what we are attracted to, how we relate to others, what talents we use to make money, as well as our core values and creeds. Some of us will have to confront insecurities and lower self-esteem during the retrograde.

Many people change their attitudes, ideals, ethics, public image, dress code, and philosophies. It is a good time to get out of contracts that are not good for you.

Venus retrograde is a time when people are more blunt, combative, and lack diplomacy. You will also see a great deal of awkwardness on the world stage between diplomats as well as in the court system.

When Venus is retrograde, it is not recommended to get engaged or married, form business partnerships, buy art, make investments, start lawsuits, or spend money. If you are planning a cosmetic operation or an IVF, better wait for Venus to forget about her rejection and land her dragon safely on greener pastures.

Venus retrograde in Gemini specifically deals with how we communicate with our significant others, as well as relationships with business partners, siblings, and relatives. During Venus' long journey in Gemini (April 3 to August 7), we have the opportunity to connect beauty, art and finance with communication, technology, and business. Letters merge with notes, numbers with colors. Your art can be communicative and your communication artistic.

The retrograde can bring back money owed to you and reconnect you with a talent or a project you have left in the past. You might also reconnect to a close friend from school.

Because of her retrograde motion, Venus will spend April to early August in your house of sexuality, passion, and transformation, precisely the energies associated with your sign.

This means that you will be able to tap into these qualities, especially through a partner, art, design, and beauty. This is a great time to reconnect to a talent or artistic hobby you might have had in the past. The more intimacy you can create around you, the more income and self-worth you will generate. This could also mean that your partner might get a promotion or generate more money.

From November 21 to December 15, Venus is in your sign. You feel attractive, desired, and lucky. You channel the qualities of beauty, diplomacy, and tact. You appear sympathetic, kind, and might even feel more flirtatious. Be careful not to overdo it and succumb to vanity and largesse.

Mars
Assertion, Passion, Leadership

Mars, your ruler, is the engine of the zodiac. He is hot, driven, passionate, aggressive, explosive, and impulsive. He was named "Father of Rome" and he might have had his origins as a god of vegetation. Mars is still associated with spring and seeds. Even in Genesis 1:12, we find a trace of the connection between Mars and vegetation. On the third day of creation, that is on "Martes" (day of Mars), God created vegetation and seeds, which is at least something monotheists and pagan agree on.

This year, Mars will be traveling from June 28 until the end of the year in Aries, even though he usually spends just a few weeks in a sign. Mars, the god of war, is the ruler of Aries, the sign of warfare. This does not necessarily mean war is upon us, but it does indicate there will be a great deal of strife, discord, and conflict. Astrology, like anything else in life, is relative — you might feel more belligerent than your usual self. Call it an Incredible-Hulk aspect: things, people, situations will drive us MADDDDDD!

This year, Mars will be retrograde in Aries between September 9 and November 14. When Mars is retrograding, it is not a very auspicious time to start big projects with large investments. It is not a good time for surgery and medical procedures. Neither is it recommended to start an intimate or sexual relationship. Avoid buying big machinery, making large investments, or starting wars or lawsuits. It is a more dangerous time, since wars, conflicts, explosions, and terror seem to follow Mars. After all, Mars' moons are called Phobos (fear) and Deimos (terror). If you need to fight, let the opponent fire the first bullet. Whoever starts a war with Mars retrograde, loses.

The Brexit referendum took place during Mars retrograde in Aquarius, the sign of government and community. And what happened right after? Oops, regret. What have we done? That is a typical Mars retrograde reaction. Another infamous example is the non-aggression treaty signed by Nazi Germany and the Soviets before WWII (Molotov-Ribbentrop). It was also a Mars retrograde station, and, obviously did not last long. Watch out for what agreements or treaties you sign, what you agree to, what you promise to do, what you fight for, and what you are willing to do to satiate your passions. Mars retrograde is a good time to review your past strategies, rethink your battles and wars, change direction in leadership, and admit that you were wrong. Take extra care between October 13 and November 4, since both Mars and Mercury are retrograde. Miscommunications and misunderstandings can easily flare into full-fledged wars.

Below is a list of Mars transits through the signs that can help you determine where to focus your energy.

However, remember that even the best fighters need a general. Make sure you pace yourself and control your inner warrior. Since Mars is your planet, anywhere he goes, so do you.

January 3 to February 16 – Mars in Sagittarius: This Mars transit gives you a good start to the year with energy and passion for travel, study, and authenticity. Mars can help you jumpstart a new source of income as he is traveling in your house of money, talents, and self-worth. Mars can be like a general fighting a financial campaign. It is a good time to fight for your values and ask for a promotion or a raise.

February 16 to March 30 – Mars in Capricorn: Mars through the filter of Capricorn exhibits his best qualities. He is the trained martial artist, fighting only when it is needed and he can easily win. However, be aware that Mercury retrograde might slow things down. Mars is traveling in your house of communication and relatives. He gives you a boost of energy in study, writing, and marketing, which is what you need now. However, he can create some challenges or a need to work with relatives and siblings.

March 30 to May 13 – Mars in Aquarius: This is a good time to fight for your ideals, for your group and company, and come to the rescue of a friend in need. However, it can also create conflict with certain friends or people in your company. Mars is in your house of home and family and while he can bring you energy to fix your home, renovate, or even move, he can also manifest as discord and fights with family members.

May 13 to June 28 – Mars in Pisces: With this transit of Mars, you have to make sure you are getting enough sleep and rest. Give time for your immune system to recover. It is a good time for interval fasting as well as for meditation and yoga. Two powerful eclipses, as well as Venus retrograde, are taking place and it can be intense out there. It is a good time for physical activities near or in water such as swimming, surfing, rowing, hiking / running / cycling by a body of water. Mars is plowing through your house of children, love, and happiness. Mars wants you to be active, entertaining, and fun. Spend time outdoors and initiate recreational activities. It is a good time for a creative project or a new hobby.

June 29 – End of the Year – Mars in Aries: Mars likes to be home in Aries, the sign of his rulership. The king is back in his palace. However, it can get hot and aggressive. Mars in Aries can be domineering. So back off and don't be overly cocky or too pushy. Lead through example and not fear or intimidation. It is a good time to explore, do things you never did, ask for a raise, and put your foot down. However, remember that between September 9 and November 14, Mars is retrograde. Some delays and a pushback from life will take place. It might feel as if you are hitting the brakes after going 100 mph. Mars is in your house of diet, health, and work. This is a time to start a new exercise routine, initiate a project in work, fight for a promotion, or explore leadership roles in your workplace. Don't wait for things to happen. Make them manifest! Watch from head injuries and accidents.

Uranus - *Unpredictability, Originality, and a Touch of Chaos*

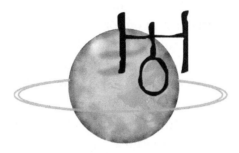

In March 2019, Uranus made his final move into Taurus, which is your opposite sign and located in your house of relationships and marriage. He will be there until 2026. It is not easy to have Uranus opposite to your Sun. People born between October 23 and November 2 might feel a need to rebel, break away from parental influence, and liberate themselves. For most Scorpios, this Uranus will feel like an awakening and a need to get out of oppressive relationships or partnerships. This aspect happens once in 84 years, so it is very rare and intense even for you. There could also be unpredictable lawsuits, or suddenly you find yourself fighting with an antagonist or someone or something that feels like an enemy. You could pick up a cause or join a group that fights for something meaningful. In addition, you or your partner might express the need for more freedom, or the need to redefine the nature of the relationship.

If you don't have a partner, you might find yourself dealing with a great deal of jokers and fools, mad professors, and yet fun, exciting, spontaneous, ingenious people who come in and out of your life.

Uranus favors technology, innovation, and science. Maybe you can think of a great new application or an e-commerce business idea. It is also a good time to redo your website, give your Facebook page a face lift, and connect to social media. Maybe even a meet with a new partner through a community, virtual or real.

Your Hebrew Letter and Tarot Card:

Since 2020 is the year of 22, below is the Major Arcana card associated with your sign as well as the Hebrew letter. You can use the letter and place it inside the diamond in your meditation. The letter can also be used like a talisman to help you connect to your archetype. You will notice that in many cases, the letter's shape resembles its meaning. In my book *Cosmic Navigator*, you can find more information about the connection between the Hebrew letters and the zodiac signs.

Tarot: DEATH

Hebrew letter: Nun

נ

The letter means "a snake." Scorpio is the only sign with three glyphs representing its essence: scorpion, snake, eagle. The snake sheds its skin and symbolizes transformation, healing, and magic.

Summary:

2020 is an intense year even for you, the sign of intensity. The main focus this year is communication: what is your message, who do you need to deliver this message, and what medium will best serve? The message can be information, data, emotions, creative, fiction, no-fiction, technical, or psychic. In addition, 2020 is a year where you have to promote yourself and learn how to market your talents and abilities.

SAGITTARIUS

New Karmic Cycle:
Values, Self-Worth, and Finance

In 2020, you continue investigating your true talents, and
how, with the help of a healthy dose of self-worth, you
can increase your income. Everyone thinks that you are
the happy-go-lucky sign. Everyone assumes you are in
love with life and with yourself, but since 2015, it has not
been easy. While it is true that Jupiter was on your side
in 2019, you also had to experience a great deal of harsh
life lessons that have reduced your sense of self-worth
and maybe even put a dent on your finances. In January
2020, Saturn, Jupiter, and Pluto are conjunct and start a
new cycle that, with the help of discipline, focus, and
planning, can dramatically improve your finances and
even unearth new revenue streams. Saturn can help you
rectify your finances and Pluto can aid in resurrecting
hidden talents. However, the price of Pluto's help is a
death or an end of the old way of making money.
You must let go of whatever patterns hold you back in
your personal life, since they also manifest in your
profession.

From mid-March to early July, Saturn momentarily shifts gears and moves into Aquarius, the sign that rules your house of relatives, communication, business, and contracts. You will have to deal with these aspects of life and face some challenges, which will become dominant in your life again in 2021 and 2022. However, in these years, you will also have Jupiter helping create new opportunities for connections, businesses, and marketing.

The North Node moves to Gemini, your opposite sign, from June 2020 to the end of 2021 which places the South Node in your sign. That means that you, along with the rest of humanity, will have to let go of the negative aspects of your sign: over-optimism, fanaticism, zealotry, over-religiosity, gluttony, and being too preachy or sanctimonious. There will be a great deal of discussion about what is the difference between *my* truth, *your* truth, and *the* truth. The next two years is a good time for you to be a bit less Sagittarius and more Gemini, your complementary sign. That means focusing on writing, marketing yourself, communicating, connecting people, and most importantly, breathing. Since the North Node is moving in June to your house of relationships, it means being less focused on yourself and more on your partner or relationships.

Venus, the goddess of love, travels from April to August in your house of relationships. This could bring a new love, or color an old love with more sparkle. When Venus is retrograde in May and June, she might bring back an old-flame or reconnect you to a talent you neglected in the past.

Mars travels from July to the end of the year in your house of love and happiness. This can support Venus' attempts to bring you a partner. Since Mars is also the planet of seeds, be aware that whether you plan it or not, a baby may want to reincarnate through you.

Uranus, the planet of unpredictability, is in your house of health and work, so watch your diet and routine as it might become disrupted. Uranus wants you to connect to new ways of doing your work. It is a great year for an update, upgrade, connecting to technology, or innovation. 2020 is also a good year to join new groups in your work and professional life.

The Six Eclipses
Your Emotional Landscape

In Part I, I shared the meaning behind the eclipses and their Sabian symbols and paths. To make it easier, I have included some of that information below, as well as the way the eclipses manifest in your sign.

The eclipses this year are a mixed bag for you. As you will see below, those that fall in Cancer (water sign) and Capricorn (earth sign) are a bit more challenging for you as a Fire-Bender. They create an opposition and a push-pull between your house of finance and the house of investments or other people's money. These eclipses also activate your sexuality and intimacy, forcing you to examine your passions in life. However, from June 2020 until the end of 2021, the eclipses will be in your sign and in Gemini. They will ask you to look at dualities — I versus thou, mine versus yours, what I want against what we want.

Jan 10 / 11: Penumbral Lunar eclipse in Cancer. Sabian symbol: Prima donna singing. Eclipse path: Europe, Asia, Australia, Africa, most of North America, east part of South America, Pacific, Atlantic, and Indian Oceans.

To understand the story of this eclipse, let's return to the movie analogy. The first act of your story took place during the eclipses of July 2019. The eclipse on January 10, 2020, is the second act of your film. The third and final act is performed on the eclipse of July 5, 2020. Pay attention to synchronicities or anything out of the ordinary taking place during these dates and try to link the events of the eclipses to a narrative. The eclipses fall in your house of sexuality, intimacy, and death. The process of letting go that has taken place in your life for almost a year continues. The eclipses can also help you heal from past intimacy issues or sexual problems. There is a push and pull between your finances and those of your partner in life or in work.

June 5 / 6: Penumbral Lunar eclipse in Sagittarius.
Sabian symbol: Seagulls watching a ship. Eclipse path: Europe, most of Asia, Australia, Africa, south / east South America, Pacific, Atlantic, Indian Oceans. This eclipse is the first of the Gemini-Sagittarius axial eclipses — welcome to the first eclipse connected to your sign. The North Node shifts and so does your focus. In the next 18 months, you will have to learn how to let go of yourself in order to find a partner or find harmony in your relationships.

This does not imply self-annihilation; it simply suggests that you have to try to put your partner first in order to spiritually evolve.

June 21: Solar Annular Solstice eclipse in Cancer.
Sabian symbol: A sailor ready to hoist a new flag to
replace an old one. Eclipse path: south / east Europe,
most of Asia, north Australia, most of Africa, Pacific and
Indian Oceans. In addition, this eclipse takes place
during a retrograde bonanza: Mercury, Venus, Pluto,
Saturn, Pallas, and Jupiter are all in retrograde motion.
This means their expression is more internal and it will
feel like you are a passenger in a car driven by a very
bad driver. Take extra care in how you relate to and
communicate with lovers, friends and authority figures.
This Solar eclipse can bring about a swift new beginning
in healing, transformation, works in production, or joint
financial affairs. You are going through an open-soul
operation. Expect a great deal of change in your life as
you shed blocks and obstacles.

July 4 / 5: Penumbral Lunar eclipse in Capricorn. Sabian
symbol: An ancient bas-relief carved in granite. Eclipse
path: south / west Europe, most of Africa, North
America, South America, Pacific, Atlantic, and Indian
Oceans. This eclipse is the mirror image of the Lunar
eclipse of January 10 and therefore is the climax of
whatever you started in July 2019.

Mercury is retrograde during this eclipse, therefore, we
are still in danger of miscommunication and regretting
our actions and / or choices. This eclipse can be a bit
difficult on your finances, so be extra careful. It is the last
eclipse that falls in your house of intimacy and sexuality.

Nov 29 / 30: Penumbral Lunar eclipse in Gemini. Sabian symbol: Quiver filled with arrows. Eclipse path: Europe, most of Asia, Australia, North America, South America, Pacific and Atlantic Oceans. The eclipse continues the exploration of what is true and what is false. It is a time to change the way we learn and teach. The eclipse brings to the foreground opposition between you and your partner and the need to find harmony and peace with your significant others.

Dec 14: Total Solar eclipse in Sagittarius. Sabian symbol: Blue bird standing at the door of the house. Eclipse path: South Africa, South America, Pacific, Atlantic and Indian Oceans. This is a powerful eclipse that begins a new journey in education, travel, and publishing. This is your eclipse as it is a New Moon in your sign. You might encounter an inspiring mentor or become one for someone else. This eclipse is a good time for rebranding, changing your image, making new business cards, and renewing your digital footprint.

Mercury Retrograde - *The Trickster*

Mercury is the trickster. Even when he is cruising direct through the heavens, he likes to pull practical jokes. I always thought that this was his compensation for delivering messages. When Mercury is retrograde, his tricks and ruses go to the next level. Of course, Mercury does not really retrograde, but from an earthly vantage point, Mercury does look as if he is going backwards three or four times a year for about three weeks. Mercury, the messenger of the gods and goddesses, represents the archetype of communication, connections, computers, emails, texts, messages, directions, information, data, cables, Wi-Fi, the nervous system, and breathing. During Mercury retrograde, all these aspects of life are reversed, malfunctioning. Error messages, delays, accidents, mishaps, misspelling, and glitches plague the earth.

During Mercury retrograde, it is not recommended to start new long-term projects, sign documents, make large purchases, get married, start marketing campaigns, publish, inaugurate locations or homes, or release new products. Communications of all sorts are slower and more challenging. Computers crash; stock markets turn volatile; flights are delayed; traffic is worse than usual; accidents occur more often; and Murphy's Law takes hold of all aspects of our lives. If you need to fly during Mercury retrograde, make sure you do your online check-in and allow more time to reach the airport. Try to avoid overscheduling yourself or being overly critical and demanding, and pay attention to your diet and food intake.

If you must start a new project, be as mindful as you can. Pay attention to small details and read in-between the lines if you must sign a document. Rewrite your emails; edit your texts; and think before you speak or post. In fact, it is better if you spend more time listening than talking. Life does not come to a halt during Mercury retrograde. You can still achieve a great deal during his retrograde. It is like going on a vacation in Sweden in the winter: It can still be fun, just make sure you take a coat. However, Mercury retrograde is a great time to edit, redo, reexamine yourself and your path, revisit old projects, and find lost objects. Try to focus on activities that have the prefix *re* – reevaluate, reedit, redo, reexamine, reconnect, regenerate, revisit, re-imagine, etc.

Mercury is a liminal god and also a shadow-walker, a psychopomp, and a wizard (Hermetic studies are named after his Greek name). Jung identified him as the god of synchronicities, and it is true that during Mercury retrograde there are far more synchronicities and meaningful coincidences. Yes, you might have made it to the wrong place for your meeting, but there you bump into someone you have been unable to track for ages. And yes, you might arrive to the appointment at 9 AM instead of 9 PM, but because of that "mistake," you may have avoided a terrible accident.

Mercury retrograde is always challenging for you since it is the ruler of Gemini, your opposite sign. This means that, during Mercury retrograde significant issues between you and your partners come into the open, or perhaps you experience the typical mercurial glitches with your partner. Since you are a Fire-Bender and these retrogrades are in water signs, life may be more emotional than with retrogrades in the other elements.

1st Retro: February 16 – March 10. From Feb 16 to March 4, Mercury is retrograde in Pisces which squares your Sun which means you will be forced into an action you might not want to carry out. The retrograde is in your house of home and family and family members can be a bit more difficult.

From March 4 to March 10, Mercury is retrograde in Aquarius, which is your house of relatives, siblings, and communication. This may cause issues with contracts and other types of documents, or in relationships with relatives or neighbors.

2nd Retro: June 18 – July 12. Mercury retrogrades in Cancer. Be careful with this one, since it takes place during the powerful eclipse on June 21st. Be extra careful with investments and in dealing with other people's money. This retrograde falls in your house of death, sexuality, and intimacy and these aspects can feel a bit stressed.

3rd Retro: Oct 13 – Nov 3. Mercury is retrograde in Scorpio between October 13 and October 28, when Mars is also retrograde. This double retro motion also happened in July and August 2018. You can look back and see what happened then and maybe avoid similar mistakes. This retrograde is especially intense as it falls in your house of letting go, pain, and suffering. However, if you chill out, dedicate time for deep meditations, and shift to a lower gear, you can actually benefit from dreams, intuition, and even memories from past lives.

From October 28 to November 3 Mercury will be retrograde in Libra, which falls in your house of friends and community. If you work in a large organization, there could be a great deal of political issues or miscommunication with coworkers, friends, and colleagues.

Venus
Love, Pleasure, Art and Finance

Everyone loves Venus. Actually, what I just wrote, to an ancient Greek, would sound like a redundancy, since Venus embodies love and who does not love *love*?

But this year, it will be harder to love love, since Venus will be retrograding in Gemini between May 13 to June 25. She will be riding the Dragon, North Node, like an angry Khaleesi, who was just rejected by her John Snow. Venus goes retrograde once in 18 months for 40 days and 40 nights. It is a time we should dedicate to reevaluating our relationships, what we attract and what we are attracted to, how we relate to others, what talents we use to make money as well as our core values and creeds. Some of us will have to confront insecurities and lower self-esteem during the retrograde. Many people change their attitudes, ideals, ethics, public image, dress code, and philosophies.

It is a good time to get out of contracts that are not good for you. Venus retrograde is a time when people are more blunt, combative, and lack diplomacy. You will also see a great deal of awkwardness on the world stage between diplomats as well as in the court system.

When Venus is retrograde, it is not recommended to get engaged or married, form business partnerships, buy art, make investments, start lawsuits, or spend money. If you are planning a cosmetic operation or an IVF, better wait for Venus to forget about her rejection and land her dragon safely on greener pastures.

Venus retrograde in Gemini specifically deals with how we communicate with our significant others, as well as relationships with business partners, siblings, and relatives. During Venus' long journey in Gemini (April 3 to August 7), we have the opportunity to connect beauty, art and finance with communication, technology, and business. Letters merge with notes, numbers with colors. Your art can be communicative and your communication artistic.

The retrograde can bring back money owed to you and reconnect you with a talent or a project you have neglected from the past. You might also reconnect to a close friend from school.

Because of her retrograde motion, Venus will spend April to early August in your house of relationships and marriage. You may see that you cannot escape from the need to settle down and find a like-minded, free-spirited, yet committed partner in work or and in life. Venus is the archetype of love and relationships and she is spending a lot of time in your house of relationship this year. She expects some action! While she is retrograding (May and June) people from your past might resurface. If you do want to revisit an old-flame, make sure there has been a big change, a death — symbolic or real — in your life or theirs. There has to have been a major change in both of you for you guys to try again. It is not a good time to start a relationship between May 13 and June 25, so please, take your time.

Venus is in your sign for the last two weeks of the year, beginning on December 15. You feel attractive, desired, and lucky. You channel the qualities of beauty, diplomacy, and tact. You appear sympathetic, kind, and might even feel more flirtatious. Be careful not to overdo it and fall into vanity and pride.

Mars
Assertion, Passion, Leadership

Mars is the engine of the zodiac. He is hot, driven, passionate, aggressive, explosive, and impulsive. The Romans saw him as their father and some scholars trace his mythological origins to a god of vegetation. Mars is still associated with spring and seeds. Even in Genesis 1:12, we find a hint of the connection between Mars and vegetation. On the third day of creation, that is on "Martes" (day of Mars), God created vegetation and seeds: "Let the earth burst forth with every sort of grass and seed-bearing plant, and fruit trees with seeds inside the fruit, so that these seeds will produce the kinds of plants and fruits they came from." And so it was, and God was pleased.

Between June 28 and the end of the year, Mars will be traveling in Aries. This is abnormal as usually Mars spends about six weeks, not six months, in a sign. Mars, the god of war, is the ruler of Aries, the sign of warfare. Yes, this can raise the probability of armed conflict, cyber-attacks, and other displays of aggression.

This transit indicates there will be a great deal of strife, discord, and conflict. Astrology, like anything else in life is relative, so you might feel more belligerent than your usual self. Call it an Incredible-Hulk aspect: things, people, and situations will drive you MADDDDDD!

This year, Mars will be retrograde in Aries between September 9 and November 14. When Mars is retrograding, it is not a very auspicious time to start big projects with large investments. It is not a good time for surgery and medical procedures unless urgent. Neither is it recommended to start an intimate or sexual relationship. Avoid buying big machinery, making large investments, or starting wars or lawsuits. It is a more dangerous time, since wars, conflicts, explosions, and terror seem to follow Mars. After all, Mars' moons are called Phobos (fear) and Deimos (terror). If you need to fight, let the opponent fire the first bullet. Whoever starts a war with Mars retrograde, loses.

The Brexit referendum took place during Mars retrograde in Aquarius, the sign of government and community. And what happened right after? Oops, regret. What have we done? That is a typical Mars retrograde reaction. Another infamous example is the non-aggression treaty signed by Nazi Germany and the Soviets before WWII (Molotov-Ribbentrop). It was also a Mars retrograde station, and, obviously did not last long.

Even though Mars retrograde is not a Mercury retrograde, avoid signing treaties or agreements that deal with action, wars, or campaigns. Be mindful of what you agree to do, what you promise to carry out, what you fight for, and what you are willing to do to satiate your passions. Mars retrograde is a good time to review your past strategies, rethink your battles and wars, change direction in leadership, and admit that you were wrong.

Take extra care between October 13 and November 4, since both Mars and Mercury are retrograde. Miscommunications and misunderstandings can easily flare into full-fledged wars.

Below is a list of Mars transits through the signs that can help you determine where to focus your energy. However, remember that even the best fighters need a general. Make sure you pace yourself and control your inner warrior.

January 3 to February 16 – Mars in Sagittarius: This Mars transit gives you a good start to the year with energy and passion for travel, study and authenticity. As you can see, Mars' first station this year is in your sign. This should give you a big boost this year and is a sign of a lot of action in 2020. **February 16 to March 30 – Mars in Capricorn:** Mars through the filter of Capricorn exhibits his best qualities. He is the trained martial artist, fighting only when it is needed and he can easily win.

However, be aware that Mercury retrograde might slow things down. Mars can bring a new source of income as he is traveling in your house of money, talents, and self-worth. Mars can be like a general fighting a financial campaign. It is a good time to fight for your values and ask for a promotion or a raise.

March 30 to May 13 – Mars in Aquarius: This is a good time to fight for your ideals, for your group and company, and come to the rescue of a friend in need. However, it can also create conflict with certain friends or people in your company. Mars is traveling in your house of communication and relatives. He gives you a boost of energy in study, writing, and contracts. However, he can create some challenges or a need to work with relatives and siblings.

May 13 to June 28 – Mars in Pisces: With this transit of Mars, you have to make sure you are getting enough sleep and rest. Give time for your immune system to recover. It is a good time for interval fasting as well as for meditation and yoga. Two powerful eclipses, as well as Venus retrograde, are taking place and it can be intense out there. It is a good time for physical activities near or in water such as swimming, surfing, rowing, hiking / running / cycling by a body of water. Mars is in your house of home and family, and while he can bring you energy to fix your home, renovate, or even move, he can also manifest as discord and fights with family members.

June 29 – End of the Year – Mars in Aries: Mars likes to be home in Aries, the sign of his rulership. The king is back in his palace. However, it can get hot and aggressive. Mars in Aries can be domineering. So back off and don't be overly cocky or too pushy. Lead through example and not fear or intimidation. It is a good time to explore, do things you never did, ask for a raise, and put your foot down. However, remember that between September 9 and November 14, Mars is retrograde. Some delays and a pushback from life will take place.

It might feel as if you are hitting the brakes after going 100 mph. Mars is plowing through your house of children, love, and happiness. Mars wants you to be active, entertaining, and fun. Spend time outdoors and initiate recreational activities; it is also a good time for a creative project or a new hobby. You can see the main theme of 2020: Venus is in your house of relationships and Mars is in your house of love. Something is opening your heart.

Uranus - *Unpredictability, Originality, and a Touch of Chaos*

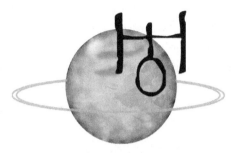

In March 2019, Uranus made his final move into Taurus, located in your house of work, health, and diet. He will transit in this house until 2026, disrupting and awakening your work life as well as the need to change your diet and work on your health. Uranus is not easy to handle. He is like a wild horse that refuses to be tamed. One day, he pretends to be docile ready to be saddled. The next day, he bucks you off. The placement of Uranus in Taurus can manifest as unexpected situations in health, or sudden injuries and ailments that manifest as quickly as they disappear. Uranus can also bring about sudden changes in your workplace or with employees and coworkers. He is the planet of revolutions and rebellion. So be aware that changes are coming to your routine. Uranus favors technology, innovation, and science. Maybe you can think of a great new application or an e- commerce business idea.

Your Hebrew Letter and Tarot Card:

Since 2020 is the year of 22, below is the Major Arcana card associated with your sign as well as the Hebrew letter. You can use the letter and place it inside the diamond in your meditation. The letter can also be used like a talisman to help you connect to your archetype. You will notice that in many cases, the letter's shape resembles its meaning. In my book *Cosmic Navigator*, you can find more information about the connection between the Hebrew letters and the zodiac signs.

Tarot: TEMPERANCE

Hebrew letter: Samech

The letter means "trust" and "support." The letter's shape resembles a pillow or a chair's backrest. Sagittarius draws its optimism from trust and the knowledge that life supports them.

Summary:

2020 is an intense year as the eclipses are focused in your house of death, sexuality, intimacy and transformation. There is a great deal of work you need to do on your self-worth and talents in order to change or add to your income. In addition, this is the year where love is in the air with Venus, North Node, and Mars, converging in your house of relationship and love. Go get them, centaurs!

CAPRICORN

New Karmic Cycle:
Complete Makeover

2020 is a one-in-a-million kind of year for you Capricorn. If you thought 2019 was intense, 2020 will break the galactic record. In 2019, you had a lot of special guest stars including Saturn, your ruler, Pluto, the Lord of Death, and the eclipses. This year, two major things are happening that add a bit of drama:

From December 2019, Jupiter, the planet of opportunities and expansion, has moved into your sign. This cycle occurs once in twelve years (2008, 1996, etc.) and it is great news for your clan. Jupiter brings a breeze of fresh air in a time you need it most and will improve your health, mood, energy level, and help you rebrand and reinvent yourself. Jupiter can bring about a good change in your path, a new opportunity for self-improvement, and a great deal of luck and synchronicities.

On January 10, we are having an eclipse in your sign as well as one of the most dreaded conjunctions in a generation: Saturn and Pluto come together in your sign. The last time these two were in conjunction was in 1982. It is recommended to look back and see what happened to you at that time, that is, if you were alive. However, the last time Saturn and Pluto were conjunct in your sign was over 250 years ago! Conjunctions are always an initiation of a cycle and it is taking place in your house of body and personality. Watch your health and don't take extra risks — physically, mentally, and emotionally. I know you are the sign of caution and responsibility, and yet I do find it necessary to warn you. It is not all sadness and gloom as this conjunction can be not just a change of direction in life but the building of a grand new infrastructure of highways to take you to your true destination. This conjunction is a mega-transformation that might feel like a death and a resurrection.

The North Node will be moving in June away from your opposite sign, Cancer, into Gemini and it will be easier to handle the lunatic energies of the Moon. The eclipses will take place in your house of work, health, and diet, as well as the house of letting go. This means that in June and again in December, there will be some changes in your work, routine, diet, and how you serve humanity. Venus will also be staying in your house of work for a long period this year (April – early August), which can bring new creative and exciting possibilities in your work.

Uranus, the Joker and Fool, is hiking in your house of love and happiness. He could bring sudden changes with your love life, creativity, and children. If you have teenage kids, well, they might act in a rebellious way. Since Uranus is unpredictable and somewhat chaotic, he can add some colors to your life. There could be unexpected falling-in-love situation. If you are married or in a partnership, think twice before acting in extra-marital affairs since Uranus is not always to be trusted. He shows up suddenly and disappears just as fast.

The last six months of the year are colored by Mars traveling in your house of home and family. You might feel a need to spend more time or effort in your home or with family members. It is not a bad time for a renovation or change of location, but be extra careful when Mars is retrograde between September and mid-November. Also, remember that Mars in Aries is squaring your sign, which means you might be prompted into taking action with real estate or family which you might later regret.

Overall, 2020 is a very dramatic year that will force a change in your usual status-quo-keeping mentality. Embrace the change and don't resist it.

The Six Eclipses
Your Emotional Landscape

In Part I, I shared the meaning behind the eclipses and their Sabian symbols and paths. To make it easier, I have included some of that information below, as well as the way the eclipses manifest in your sign.

The eclipses have been in your sign from the beginning of 2019, propelling things faster in your life, especially in relation to your path in life, identity, and relationships. Until June 2020, you will continue this tango between your needs and your partner's desires. From June 2020 to the end of 2021, you will shift gears and experience the lunations in your house of health and work as well as the house of past lives, mysticism, and hospitals. Around the dates of the eclipses, you will have to let go of something in your work or your diet in order to allow your life to run more smoothly. During the eclipses, it is recommended to spend more time alone or practice more yoga and meditation. Retreats of all kinds could be also helpful in channeling the dragon.

Jan 10 / 11: Penumbral Lunar eclipse in Cancer. Sabian symbol: Prima donna singing. Eclipse path: Europe, Asia, Australia, Africa, most of North America, east part of South America, Pacific, Atlantic, and Indian Oceans. To understand the story of this eclipse, let's return to the movie analogy. The first act of your story took place during the eclipses of July 2019. The eclipse on January 10, 2020, is the second act of your film. The third and final act is performed on the eclipse of July 4, 2020. Pay attention to synchronicities or anything out of the ordinary taking place during these dates and try to link the events of the eclipses to a narrative. The eclipses fall in your house of relationships and marriage. You have to tread very carefully with your partners in work and in life. The eclipses can also expose someone who wants to harm you. Be extra careful with lawsuits.

June 5 / 6: Penumbral Lunar eclipse in Sagittarius.
Sabian symbol: Seagulls watching a ship. Eclipse path: Europe, most of Asia, Australia, Africa, south / east South America, Pacific, Atlantic, Indian Oceans. This eclipse is the first of the new cycle and creates an opposition between the duty to serve and work with others and the need for quiet and isolation. Since the eclipse is happening in the house of hospital, jails, and confinement, please be extra careful.

June 21: Solar Annular Solstice eclipse in Cancer.
Sabian symbol: A sailor ready to hoist a new flag to replace an old one. Eclipse path: south / east Europe, most of Asia, north Australia, most of Africa, Pacific and Indian Ocean. In addition, this eclipse takes place during

a retrograde bonanza: Mercury, Venus, Pluto, Saturn, Pallas, and Jupiter are all in retrograde motion. This means their expression is more internal and it will feel like you are a passenger in a car driven by a very bad driver. Take extra care with how you talk to, relate to, and communicate with lovers, friends, and authority figures. This Solar eclipse can bring about a new exciting relationship or someone with whom you could create a harmonious and profitable partnership. This eclipse represents a new beginning to how you view and deal with relationships of all kinds.

July 4 / 5: Penumbral Lunar eclipse in Capricorn. Sabian symbol: An ancient bas-relief carved in granite. Eclipse path: south / west Europe, most of Africa, North America, South America, Pacific, Atlantic, and Indian Oceans. This eclipse is the mirror image of the Lunar eclipse of January 10 and therefore is the climax of whatever started in July 2019. Mercury is retrograde during this eclipse, therefore, we are still in danger of miscommunication and regretting our actions and / or choices.

This eclipse falls in your sign and is the mirror image of whatever took place in your life in the end of December 2019. You might be extra moody and emotional. So please cut some slack to people around you.

Nov 29 / 30: Penumbral Lunar eclipse in Gemini. Sabian symbol: Quiver filled with arrows. Eclipse path: Europe, most of Asia, Australia, North America, South America,

Pacific and Atlantic Oceans. The eclipse continues the exploration of what is true and what is false. It is a time to change the way we learn and teach. There could be some issues with your health or work and, if you are an employer, you might need to let go of some employees. There could be a need for adjustments in your routine and diet.

Dec 14: Total Solar eclipse in Sagittarius. Sabian symbol: Blue bird standing at the door of the house. Eclipse path: South Africa, South America, Pacific, Atlantic and Indian Oceans. This is a powerful eclipse that begins a new journey in education, travel, and publishing. You might encounter an inspiring mentor or become one for someone else. This eclipse can bring you some gifts from a past lifetime, maybe someone you were very connected with in a previous life, or a skill or talent that can be retrieved. It is a good time to start new charity work.

Mercury Retrograde - *The Trickster*

Mercury is the trickster. Even when he is cruising direct through the heavens, he likes to pull practical jokes. I always thought that this was his compensation for delivering messages. When Mercury is retrograde, his tricks and ruses go to the next level. Of course, Mercury does not really retrograde, but from an earthly vantage point, Mercury does look as if he is going backwards three or four times a year for about three weeks. Mercury, the messenger of the gods and goddesses, represents the archetype of communication, connections, computers, emails, texts, messages, directions, information, data, cables, Wi-Fi, the nervous system, and breathing. During Mercury retrograde, all these aspects of life are reversed, malfunctioning. Error messages, delays, accidents, mishaps, misspelling, and glitches plague the earth.

During Mercury retrograde, it is not recommended to start new long-term projects, sign documents, make

large purchases, get married, start marketing campaigns, publish, inaugurate locations or homes, or release new products. Communications of all sorts are slower and more challenging. Computers crash; stock markets turn volatile; flights are delayed; traffic is worse than usual; accidents occur more often; and Murphy's Law takes hold of all aspects of our lives. If you need to fly during Mercury retrograde, make sure you do your online check-in and allow more time to reach the airport. Try to avoid overscheduling yourself or being overly critical and demanding. Also pay attention to your diet and food intake.

If you must start a new project, be as mindful as you can. Pay attention to small details and read in-between the lines if you must sign a document. Rewrite your emails; edit your texts; and think before you speak or post. In fact, it is better if you spend more time listening than talking. Life does not come to a halt during Mercury retrograde. You can still achieve a great deal during his retrograde. It is like going on a vacation in Sweden in the winter: It can still be fun, just make sure you take a coat. However, Mercury retrograde is a great time to edit, redo, reexamine yourself and your path, revisit old projects, and find lost objects. Try to focus on activities that have the prefix *re* – reevaluate, reedit, redo, reexamine, reconnect, regenerate, revisit, re-imagine, etc. Mercury is a liminal god and also a shadow-walker, a psychopomp, and a wizard (Hermetic studies are named after his Greek name). Jung identified him as the god of synchronicities, and it is true that during Mercury retrograde there are far more synchronicities and meaningful coincidences. Yes, you might have made it to the wrong place for your meeting, but there you bump into someone you have been unable to track for ages. And yes, you might arrive to the appointment at 9 AM instead of 9 PM, but because of that "mistake," you may have avoided a terrible accident.

Mercury retrograde is never easy for the typical Capricorn, who is known for planning everything, even their next lifetime. And so, when Mercury comes and shuffles the best made plans, it pisses you off. This year, the retrogrades are mainly happening in water signs, which as an Earth-Bender, is easier for you to handle. **1st Retro: February 16 – March 10.** From Feb 16 to March 4 Mercury is retrograde in Pisces. This is interesting, since it is happening in your house of communication. So, there you have it, the planet of communication, going backward in your house of communication in Pisces, a sign famous for its confusion. Be careful of a relapse, or falling into past negative patterns of thoughts and communication. However, it is a rare opportunity to receive messages from above, to give and receive healing, and tap into your intuition.

From March 4 to March 10, Mercury is retrograde in Aquarius, your house of money, talents, and self-worth. Be extra careful with purchases and investments. You might feel a bit hard on yourself, but it is a good time to reconnect to money-making ideas you might have abandoned in the past, or to talents you have neglected.

2nd Retro: June 18 – July 12. Mercury retrogrades in Cancer. Be careful with this one, since it takes place during the powerful eclipse on June 21st. This can cause havoc in your house of relationships and partnership. Make sure you are OK with saying "I am sorry."

3rd Retro: Oct 13 – Nov 3. Mercury is retrograde in Scorpio between October 13 and October 28, when Mars is also retrograde. This double retro motion also happened in July and August 2018. You can look back to that time and see what happened and maybe avoid similar mistakes. This retrograde takes place in your house of friends and organizations. If you work in a company or a corporation, there might be a great deal of glitches and miscommunications around you. There could also be some problems with friends or colleagues. From October 28 to November 3 Mercury will be retrograde in Libra, which falls in your house of career and people in authority. Since this retrograde is squaring your Sun, it can force you into action and make you feel impulsive, especially when dealing with father figures or bosses. Be extra careful.

Venus
Love, Pleasure, Art and Finance

Everyone loves Venus. Actually, what I just wrote, to an ancient Greek, would sound like a redundancy, since Venus embodies love and who does not love *love*?
But this year, it will be harder to love love, since Venus will be retrograding in Gemini between May 13 to June 25. She will be riding the Dragon, North Node, like an angry Khaleesi, who was just rejected by her John Snow. Venus goes retrograde once in 18 months for 40 days and 40 nights. It is a time we should dedicate to reevaluating our relationships, what we attract and what we are attracted to, how we relate to others, what talents we use to make money, as well as our core values and creeds. Some of us will have to confront insecurities and lower self-esteem during the retrograde. Many people change their attitudes, ideals, ethics, public image, dress code, and philosophies. It is a good time to get out of contracts that are not good for you.
Venus retrograde is a time when people are more blunt, combative, and lack diplomacy. You will also see a great

deal of awkwardness on the world stage between diplomats as well as in the court system.

When Venus is retrograde, it is not recommended to get engaged or married, form business partnerships, buy art, make investments, start lawsuits, or spend money. If you are planning a cosmetic operation or an IVF, better wait for Venus to forget about her rejection and land her dragon safely on greener pastures.

Venus retrograde in Gemini specifically deals with how we communicate with our significant others, as well as relationships with business partners, siblings, and relatives. During Venus' long journey in Gemini (April 3 to August 7), we have the opportunity to connect beauty, art and finance with communication, technology, and business. Letters merge with notes, numbers with colors. Your art can be communicative and your communication artistic.

The retrograde can bring back money owed to you and reconnect you with a talent or a project you have neglected in the past. You might also reconnect to a close friend from your early school days.

Because of her retrograde motion, Venus spends April to early August in your house of health, diet, work, and service. You can see that the synchronicities of 2020 are pointing you towards changes in your work and diet. Venus is considered to be one of the benevolent planets along with Jupiter, who we already saw blessing your sign this year. This means that Venus can help you find a labor of love. She can bring magic, creativity, art, and love into your work. Try to use this period to connect in a deeper way to your coworkers and employees. Venus might even bring you someone special through your work. However, during the retrograde of May 13 to June 25 be extra careful with your relationships at work. In addition, that period can be somewhat challenging with health and diet (avoid sugary or hedonistic over-fatty food).

Sorry to say that Venus will not be visiting your sign this year. Don't be sad. She will pop back to your life in the beginning of 2021.

Mars
Assertion, Passion, Leadership

Mars is the engine of the zodiac. He is hot, driven, passionate, aggressive, explosive, and impulsive. The Romans saw him as their father and some scholars trace his mythological origins as a god of vegetation. Mars is still associated with spring and seeds. Even in Genesis 1:12, we find a hint of the connection between Mars and vegetation. On the third day of creation, that is on "Martes" (day of Mars), God created vegetation and seeds: "Let the earth burst forth with every sort of grass and seed-bearing plant, and fruit trees with seeds inside the fruit, so that these seeds will produce the kinds of plants and fruits they came from." And so it was, and God was pleased.

Between June 28 and the end of the year, Mars will be traveling in Aries. This is abnormal as usually Mars spends about six weeks, not six months, in a sign. Mars, the god of war, is the ruler of Aries, the sign of warfare. Yes, this can raise the probability of armed conflict, cyber-attacks, and other displays of aggression.

This transit indicates there will be a great deal of strife, discord, and conflict. Astrology, like anything else in life is relative— you might feel more belligerent than your usual self. Call it an Incredible-Hulk aspect: things, people, and situations will drive you MADDDDDD! This year, Mars will be retrograde in Aries between September 9 to November 14. When Mars is retrograding, it is not a very auspicious time to start big projects with large investments. It is not a good time for surgery and medical procedures unless urgent. Neither is it recommended to start an intimate or sexual relationship. Avoid buying big machinery, making large investments, or starting wars or lawsuits. It is a more dangerous time, since wars, conflicts, explosions, and terror seem to follow Mars. After all, Mars' moons are called Phobos (fear) and Deimos (terror). If you need to fight, let the opponent fire the first bullet. Whoever starts a war with Mars retrograde, loses. The Brexit referendum took place during Mars retrograde in Aquarius, the sign of government and community. And what happened right after? Oops, regret. What have we done? That is a typical Mars retrograde reaction. Another infamous example is the non-aggression treaty signed by Nazi Germany and the Soviets before WWII (Molotov-Ribbentrop). It was also a Mars retrograde station, and, obviously not last long. Even though Mars retrograde is not the same as Mercury retrograde, best to avoid signing treaty or agreements that deal with action, wars, or campaigns.

Be mindful of what you agree to do, what you promise to carry out, what you fight for, and what you are willing to do to satiate your passions. Mars retrograde is a good time to review your past strategies, rethink your battles and wars, change direction in leadership, and admit that you were wrong.

Take extra care between October 13 and November 4, since both Mars and Mercury are retrograde. Miscommunications and misunderstandings can easily flare into full-fledged wars.

Below is a list of Mars transits through the signs that can help you determine where to focus your energy.

However, remember that even the best fighters need a general. Make sure you pace yourself and control your inner warrior.

January 3 to February 16 – Mars in Sagittarius: This Mars transit gives you a good start to the year with energy and passion for travel, study, and authenticity. This is not an easy position of Mars around your birthday. Mars in the house of hospital and isolation and he might manifest as a feeling of tiredness and sadness. However, this position favors meditation, dance, yoga, and any active mystical engagement. You might have some prophetic dreams. Act upon your intuition!

February 16 to March 30 – Mars in Capricorn: Mars through the filter of Capricorn exhibits his best qualities. He is the trained martial artist, fighting only when it is needed and he can easily win. However, be aware that Mercury retrograde might slow things down.

Mars in your sign adds a great deal of intensity to the already intense year. This is a call to action, the need for a new adventure. Mars is helping you to make decisions and take action. Be careful not to overstretch yourself or overstrain.

March 30 to May 13 – Mars in Aquarius: This is a good time to fight for your ideals, for your group and company, and come to the rescue of a friend in need. However, it can also create conflict with certain friends or people in your company. Mars in your house of money can give you an energy boost to make more money or find new ways to increase your income. However, Mars can also make you feel overconfident and impulsive with your finances, so take heed.

May 13 to June 28 – Mars in Pisces: With this transit of Mars, you have to make sure you are getting enough sleep and rest. Give time for your immune system to recover. It is a good time for interval fasting as well as for meditation and yoga. Two powerful eclipses, as well as Venus retrograde, are taking place and it can be intense out there.

It is a good time for physical activities near or in water such as swimming, surfing, rowing, hiking / running / cycling by a body of water. Mars is traveling in your house of communication and relatives. He gives you a boost of energy in study, writing, and marketing yourself. However, he can create some challenges or a need to work with relatives and siblings.

June 29 – End of the Year – Mars in Aries: Mars likes to be home in Aries, the sign of his rulership. The king is back in his palace. However, it can get hot and aggressive. Mars in Aries can be domineering. So back off and don't be overly cocky or too pushy. Lead through example and not fear or intimidation. It is a good time to explore, do things you never did, ask for a raise, and put your foot down. However, remember that between September 9 and November 14, Mars is retrograde. Some delays and a pushback from life will take place. It might feel as if you are hitting the brakes after going 100 mph. Mars is in Aries, which is your square sign. It can get hot and you might find yourself being overly aggressive with family members or feel abused by someone in your family. Since Mars gives you energy, it is a good time to fix your home, renovate, or even move.

Uranus - *Unpredictability, Originality, and a Touch of Chaos*

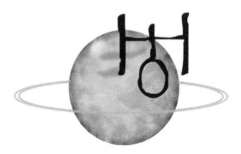

In March 2019, Uranus made his final move into Taurus, which is a fellow earth sign and therefore is easier to handle than his journey in Aries (2010-2019). Uranus transit in Taurus falls in your house of love, children, happiness, and creativity and will be there until 2026. The next few years, your children or younger people around you can help you update and upgrade yourself. Be open to leaning more about technology and new applications from younger folks. As a Capricorn, you can be a bit old-fashioned —this aspect can sometimes bring new and exciting opportunities. Uranus in the house of children can also manifest as unpredictable issues with your kids, or other children around you, either via rebellious tendencies or unexpected disruptions and changes. Again, you have to learn flexibility.

If you are in a relationship, be aware that Uranus in the house of romance can manifest as an extramarital affair which might be short-lived and somewhat rocky. So be warned. If you are single, well, Uranus might send strange, unique, ingenious, but somewhat flaky lovers your way.

Uranus favors technology, innovation, and science. Maybe you can think of a great new application or an e-commerce business idea. It is also a good time to redo your website, give your Facebook page a face lift, and connect to social media, maybe even meet with a new lover or find a creative outlet through a community, virtual or real. Uranus is the Joker, the Fool. He wants you to take a leap of faith in your love and creativity. He wants you to have fun and awaken your inner child.

Your Hebrew Letter and Tarot Card:

Since 2020 is the year of 22, below is the Major Arcana card associated with your sign as well as the Hebrew letter. You can use the letter and place it inside the diamond in your meditation. The letter can also be used like a talisman to help you connect to your archetype. You will notice that in many cases, the letter's shape resembles its meaning. In my book *Cosmic Navigator*, you can find more information about the connection between the Hebrew letters and the zodiac signs.

Tarot: THE DEVIL

Hebrew letter: Ain

The letter means "an eye." Capricorn represents practicality and can tend to be skeptical as in only believing what they can see.

Summary:

While 2020 is a powerful and intense year for all the zodiac signs, you will go through the deepest transformation. In this year, you are Atlas, holding the globe on your shoulder, since there are so many planets channeling their energies through your sign. You must be strong and yet flexible to make the changes necessary for you to grow.

AQUARIUS

New Karmic Cycle:
Soul Retrieval

For everyone in the zodiac family, 2020 is intense and somewhat challenging. For you, Aquarians, the sign that is associated with altruism, humanity, and democracy, 2020 poses two challenges. First, the fact that the conjunction of Pluto and Saturn takes place in the house of letting go, suffering, hospitals, and past lives. Second, the fact that everyone around you will be going through difficulties, which propels you to try to help them. In 2020, you are like a nun helping people heal from the plague while risking herself in the process. It is not a coincidence that in one of the most difficult years in decades, you have so many planets transiting in your house of empathy. These planets will help you channel and heal people around you and practice your water-bearing skills.

Since the end of 2017, you have been hosting Saturn, the planet of karma, in your house of pain and suffering. It does not mean that you are constantly depressed, but rather suggests that you are more aware of the pain in and around you. But the house of pain and empathy is also the house of past lives, mysticism, meditation, dreams, and imagination. While it is true that you experience pain, you also have the tools to fix, heal, and rectify suffering. In December 2019, Jupiter entered the house of pain and letting go. That is great news as it means that the cavalry is coming. This year, especially after your birthday, you will feel like there is more support, an easier flow, and an ability to let go of things that block you or hold you down. In addition, the South Node is also in your house of pain and letting go which will facilitate the release of pain and obstacles.

Another major transit that takes place this year is Saturn, your traditional ruler, moving into your sign for the first time in 30 years. This takes place between March and June, and again from the middle of December 2020 until 2023. You can go back to 1991-1993 and see what lessons and main events took place at that time. The good news is that when Saturn moves to your sign, he will have completed his journey through the house of pain and suffering and begins a new cycle.

Saturn in your sign will feel as if you carry extra responsibilities, but it is an opportunity to grow in all aspects of your life. You are also super-blessed that, right when Saturn moves into your sign, Jupiter, the planet of benevolence, is joining him. From December 2020 to the end of 2021, Jupiter will bless you with his presence, opening doors, and bestowing much positive energy. Your buckets and your emotional tank will be filled. The Great Conjunction in December 2020, which occurs once in 20 years, takes place in your sign and heralds the beginning of a new age for you as well as humanity in general. This means that the middle of this year as well as 2021-2023 offers you an opportunity to reinvent yourself and begin to manifest grand things in your life. The eclipses in June and July will help you connect to love, happiness, and children. I recommend reading and delving into what is called "positive psychology." It is a great antidote to the energies of the house of pain you are going through. Remember, you are the water-bearer and your job is to make sure humanity is on the right track and that we are kind to each other. You can only do it by leading through example.

Venus transits this year for a long period in your house of love and children. That means a chance for a grand love and some good news about your kids or creativity, especially between April and early August.

For the last six months of the year, Mars travels in your house of business, communication, and writing. This means a great deal of energy around marketing and promoting yourself. Be careful in how you communicate with people, as you might be a bit too blunt and aggressive.

In 2020, you can let go of things that, for almost 40 years, have been causing you pain and delay. It is as if Shiva, the remover of obstacles, is with you this year.

The Six Eclipses
Your Emotional Landscape

In Part I, I shared the meaning behind the eclipses and their Sabian symbols and paths. To make it easier, I have included some of that information below, as well as the way the eclipses manifest in your sign.

Since January 2019, the eclipses have been in your house of letting go, pain, and suffering, as well as the house of work, health, and diet. The eclipses might have manifested as sudden issues with your body or in your work, health and diet. However, in June 2020 until the end of 2021 the eclipses move into the houses of love, children, happiness, as well as the house of friends and community. Beginning in June, the South Node, which represents what you need to cut out of your life, is in your house of friends and community. Remember, as an Aquarius, your whole being is related to your community and humanity and beginning in June, for 18 months, the eclipses ask you to let go of some friends or organizations you belong to and focus more on love, creativity, and your happiness.

Jan 10 / 11: Penumbral Lunar eclipse in Cancer. Sabian symbol: Prima donna singing. Eclipse path: Europe, Asia, Australia, Africa, most of North America, east part of South America, Pacific, Atlantic, and Indian Oceans. To understand the story of this eclipse, let's return to the movie analogy. The first act of your story took place during the eclipses of July 2019. The eclipse on January 10, 2020, is the second act of your film. The third and final act is performed on the eclipse of July 4, 2020. Pay attention to synchronicities or anything out of the ordinary taking place during these dates and try to link the events of the eclipses to a narrative. The eclipses fall in your house of letting go and past lives. This means you might be asked once again to cut things out of your life. The eclipse can also quicken processes that have to do with employees, coworkers, health, and diet.

June 5 / 6: Penumbral Lunar eclipse in Sagittarius. Sabian symbol: Seagulls watching a ship. Eclipse path: Europe, most of Asia, Australia, Africa, south / east South America, Pacific, Atlantic, Indian Oceans. This eclipse is the first of the new Gemini-Sagittarius axial eclipses and creates an opposition between children or love and friends and companies. There may be some revelations regarding your organizations or friends. Remember, focus on your love, creativity, and developing your inner child.

June 21: Solar Annular Solstice eclipse in Cancer.
Sabian symbol: A sailor ready to hoist a new flag to
replace an old one. Eclipse path: south / east Europe,
most of Asia, north Australia, most of Africa, Pacific, and
Indian Ocean. In addition, this eclipse takes place during
a retrograde bonanza: Mercury, Venus, Pluto, Saturn,
Pallas, and Jupiter are all in retrograde motion. This
means their expression is more internal and it will feel
like you are a passenger in a car driven by a very bad
driver. Take extra care with how you talk to and
communicate with lovers, friends, and authority figures.
This is a great time to start doing yoga or any type of
movement, begin a meditation routine, or initiate a
dream journal. There might be a person or a skill coming
from a past lifetime that could kickstart something new
in your life.

July 4 / 5: Penumbral Lunar eclipse in Capricorn. Sabian
symbol: An ancient bas-relief carved in granite. Eclipse
path: south / west Europe, most of Africa, North
America, South America, Pacific, Atlantic, and Indian
Oceans. This eclipse is the mirror image of the Lunar
eclipse of January 10 and therefore is the climax of
whatever started in July 2019. Mercury is retrograde
during this eclipse; therefore we are still in danger of
miscommunication and regretting our actions and / or
choices. This is the last eclipse that will ask you to deal
with other people's suffering or pain.

Make sure you focus on preventive medicine, rest, and
relaxation, as this eclipse can manifest as health issues.

Nov 29 / 30: Penumbral Lunar eclipse in Gemini. Sabian symbol: Quiver filled with arrows. Eclipse path: Europe, most of Asia, Australia, North America, South America, Pacific and Atlantic Oceans. The eclipse continues the exploration of what is true and what is false. It is a time to change the way we learn and teach. The eclipse is helping you terminate a relationship or a friendship that does not serve you well.

Dec 14: Total Solar eclipse in Sagittarius. Sabian symbol: Blue bird standing at the door of the house. Eclipse path: South Africa, South America, Pacific, Atlantic and Indian Oceans. This is a powerful eclipse that begins a new journey in education, travel, and publishing. You might encounter an inspiring mentor or become one for someone else. This eclipse can bring you in contact with a new friend or a new community that can be beneficial.

Mercury Retrograde - *The Trickster*

Mercury is the trickster. Even when he is cruising direct through the heavens, he likes to pull practical jokes. I always thought that this was his compensation for delivering messages. When Mercury is retrograde, his tricks and ruses go to the next level. Of course, Mercury does not really retrograde, but from an earthly vantage point, Mercury does look as if he is going backwards three or four times a year for about three weeks. Mercury, the messenger of the gods and goddesses, represents the archetype of communication, connections, computers, emails, texts, messages, directions, information, data, cables, Wi-Fi, the nervous system, and breathing. During Mercury retrograde, all these aspects of life are reversed, malfunctioning. Error messages, delays, accidents, mishaps, misspelling, and glitches plague the earth.

During Mercury retrograde, it is not recommended to start new long-term projects, sign documents, make large purchases, get married, start marketing campaigns, publish, inaugurate locations or homes, or release new products. Communications of all sorts are slower and more challenging. Computers crash; stock markets turn volatile; flights are delayed; traffic is worse than usual; accidents occur more often; and Murphy's Law takes hold of all aspects of our lives. If you need to fly during Mercury retrograde, make sure you do your online check-in and allow extra time to reach the airport. Try to avoid overscheduling yourself or being overly critical and demanding. Also pay attention to your diet and food intake.

If you must start a new project, be as mindful as you can. Pay attention to small details and read in-between the lines if you must sign a document. Rewrite your emails; edit your texts; and think before you speak or post. In fact, it is better if you spend more time listening than talking. Life does not come to a halt during Mercury retrograde. You can still achieve a great deal during his retrograde. It is like going on a vacation in Sweden in the winter: It can still be fun, just make sure you take a coat. However, Mercury retrograde is a great time to edit, redo, reexamine yourself and your path, revisit old projects, and find lost objects. Try to focus on activities that have the prefix *re* – reevaluate, reedit, redo, reexamine, reconnect, regenerate, revisit, re-imagine, etc.

Mercury is a liminal god and also a shadow-walker, a psychopomp, and a wizard (Hermetic studies are named after his Greek name). Jung identified him as the god of synchronicities, and it is true that during Mercury retrograde there are far more synchronicities and meaningful coincidences. Yes, you might have made it to the wrong place for your meeting, but there you bump into someone you have been unable to track for ages. And yes, you might arrive to the appointment at 9 AM instead of 9 PM, but because of that "mistake," you may have avoided a terrible accident.

Mercury has a special connection to you, after all, you are the sign of electromagnetic waves and Mercury loves to surf those swells of information and data. However, this year Mercury is retrograde in water signs, which makes it a bit more emotional for you as you are an Air-Bender. Be especially careful when Mercury retrogrades in your sign between March 4 to March 10.

1st Retro: February 16 – March 10. From Feb 16 to March 4, Mercury retrogrades in Pisces which is your house of money, talents, and self-worth. Be extra careful with purchases and investments. You might feel a bit hard on yourself, but it is a good time to reconnect to money-making ideas you might have abandoned in the past or talents you have forgotten.

From March 4 to March 10, Mercury is retrograde in Aquarius, which is the house of your body and personality. Since it is your sign, watch your health and how you present yourself to others. There could be a great deal of confusion around first impressions and your identity.

2nd Retro: June 18 – July 12. Mercury retrogrades in Cancer. Be careful with this one, since it takes place during the powerful eclipse on June 21st. This retrograde takes place in your house of work and health. There could be a great deal of miscommunications and misunderstanding in your work and with coworkers. Watch your diet and be careful of relapsing into old addictions.

3rd Retro: Oct 13 – Nov 3. Mercury is retrograde in Scorpio between October 13 and October 28, when Mars is also retrograde. This double retro motion also happened in July and August 2018. You can go back to that time and see what happened and maybe avoid similar mistakes. This is a tough retrograde because it falls in your house of career and bosses and is squaring your sign. This means you have to think twice before you write or say anything and thrice before you act, especially when dealing with superiors. From October 28 to November 3 Mercury will be retrograde in Libra, and there could be miscommunications or issues with in-laws or when traveling with foreigners. If you are in studying in school, or teaching, take extra care.

Venus
Love, Pleasure, Art and Finance

Everyone loves Venus. Actually, what I just wrote, to an ancient Greek, would sound like a redundancy, since Venus embodies love and who does not love *love*?
But this year, it will be harder to love love, since Venus will be retrograding in Gemini between May 13 to June 25. She will be riding the Dragon, North Node, like an angry Khaleesi, who was just rejected by her John Snow.
Venus goes retrograde once in 18 months for 40 days and 40 nights. It is a time we should dedicate to reevaluating our relationships, what we attract and what we are attracted to, how we relate to others, what talents we use to make money, as well as our core values and creeds.
Some of us will have to confront insecurities and lower self-esteem during the retrograde. Many people change their attitudes, ideals, ethics, public image, dress code, and philosophies. It is a good time to get out of contracts that are not good for you.
Venus retrograde is a time when people are more blunt, combative, and lack diplomacy. You will also see a great deal of awkwardness on the world stage between diplomats as well as in the court system.

When Venus is retrograde, it is not recommended to get engaged or married, form business partnerships, buy art, make investments, start lawsuits, or spend money. If you are planning a cosmetic operation or an IVF, better wait for Venus to forget about her rejection and land her dragon safely on greener pastures.

Venus retrograde in Gemini specifically deals with how we communicate with our significant others, as well as relationships with business partners, siblings, and relatives. During Venus' long journey in Gemini (April 3 to August 7), we have the opportunity to connect beauty, art and finance with communication, technology, and business. Letters merge with notes, numbers with colors. Your art can be communicative and your communication artistic.

The retrograde can bring back money owed to you or reconnect you with a talent or a project you have neglected in the past. You might also reconnect to a close friend from school. Because of her retrograde motion, Venus will spend April to early August in your house of love, happiness, and creativity.

That is great news, since with all these transits in your house of pain and suffering, Venus, the goddess of love, spending so much time in your house of happiness is a welcome breeze of fresh air. Along with the North Node there, this transit can bring a new love, a new creative project, and a regain sense of optimism. Use these months to reconnect to a hobby or recreational activity.

However, during the retrograde period between May 13 and June 25, there could be some issues with children or with love. It is not a good time to start a new relationship, but it is a great period for revisiting an artistic project or a hobby you had a long time ago.

From December 20, 2019 to January 13, 2020, Venus transits in your sign. This is another wonderful synchronicity — during the most difficult eclipses and conjunctions of the year, you have Venus blessing you. During this time, you might feel more attractive, experience a boost in your income, and feel elevated by the intoxicating energies of the goddess of love and beauty.

Mars
Assertion, Passion, Leadership

Mars is the engine of the zodiac. He is hot, driven, passionate, aggressive, explosive, and impulsive. The Romans saw him as their father and some scholars trace his mythological origins as a god of vegetation. Mars is still associated with spring and seeds. Even in Genesis 1:12, we find a hint of the connection between Mars and vegetation. On the third day of creation, that is on "Martes" (day of Mars), God created vegetation and seeds: "Let the earth burst forth with every sort of grass and seed-bearing plant, and fruit trees with seeds inside the fruit, so that these seeds will produce the kinds of plants and fruits they came from." And so it was, and God was pleased.

Between June 28 and the end of the year, Mars will be traveling in Aries. This is abnormal as usually Mars spends about six weeks, not six months, in a sign. Mars, the god of war, is the ruler of Aries, the sign of warfare. Yes, this can raise the probability of armed conflict, cyber-attacks, and other displays of aggression. This transit indicates there will be a great deal of strife, discord, and conflict. Astrology, like anything else in life is relative — you might feel more belligerent than your usual self. Call it an Incredible-Hulk aspect: things, people, and situations will drive you MADDDDDD! This year, Mars will be retrograde in Aries between September 9 to November 14. When Mars is retrograding, it is not a very auspicious time to start big projects with large investments. It is not a good time for surgery and medical procedures unless urgent. Neither is it recommended to start an intimate or sexual relationship. Avoid buying big machinery, making large investments, or starting wars or lawsuits. It is a more dangerous time, since wars, conflicts, explosions, and terror seem to follow Mars. After all, Mars' moons are called Phobos (fear) and Deimos (terror). If you need to fight, let the opponent fire the first bullet. Whoever starts a war with Mars retrograde, loses. The Brexit referendum took place during Mars retrograde in Aquarius, the sign of government and community. And what happened right after? Oops, regret. What have we done? That is a typical Mars retrograde reaction. Another infamous example is the non-aggression treaty signed by Nazi Germany and the Soviets before WWII (Molotov-Ribbentrop). It was also a Mars retrograde station, and, obviously did not last long.

Even though Mars retrograde is not the same as Mercury retrograde, best to avoid signing treaty or agreements that deal with action, wars, or campaigns. Be mindful of what you agree to do, what you promise to carry out, what you fight for, and what you are willing to do to satiate your passions. Mars retrograde is a good time to review your past strategies, rethink your battles and wars, change direction in leadership, and admit that you were wrong.

Take extra care between October 13 and November 4, since both Mars and Mercury are retrograde. Miscommunications and misunderstandings can easily flare into full-fledged wars.

Below is a list of Mars transits through the signs that can help you determine where to focus your energy. However, remember that even the best fighters need a general. Make sure you pace yourself and control your inner warrior.

January 3 to February 16 – Mars in Sagittarius: This Mars transit gives you a good start to the year with energy and passion for travel, study, and authenticity. Mars is in your house of friends, government, and organization. It is a powerful position for Mars in your chart as you are the sign of friends and community. It means you might be called for a leadership position in your company or community. But be careful with pointless conflicts and aggression with friends.

February 16 to March 30 – Mars in Capricorn: Mars through the filter of Capricorn exhibits his best qualities. He is the trained martial artist, fighting only when it is needed and he can easily win. However, be aware that Mercury retrograde might slow things down. Mars in the house of hospital and mysticism might manifest as a feeling of tiredness and sadness. However, this position favors meditation, dance, yoga, and any active mystical engagement. You might have some prophetic dreams. Act on your intuition!

March 30 to May 13 – Mars in Aquarius: This is a good time to fight for your ideals, for your group and company, and come to the rescue of a friend in need. However, it can also create conflict with certain friends or people in your company. Mars in your sign adds a great deal of intensity to this already intense year. This is a call to action, a need for a new adventure. Mars is helping you make decisions and take action. Be careful not to overstretch yourself or overstrain.

May 13 to June 28 – Mars in Pisces: With this transit of Mars, you have to make sure you are getting enough sleep and rest. Give time for your immune system to recover. It is a good time for interval fasting as well as for meditation and yoga. Two powerful eclipses, as well as Venus retrograde, are taking place and it can be intense out there. It is a good time for physical activities near or in water such as swimming, surfing, rowing, hiking / running / cycling by a body of water. Mars in your house of money can give you a boost in energy to make more money or find new ways to increase your income. However, Mars can also make you feel overconfident and impulsive with your finances, so take heed.

June 29 – End of the Year – Mars in Aries: Mars likes to be home in Aries, the sign of his rulership. The king is back in his palace. However, it can get hot and aggressive. Mars in Aries can be domineering. So back off and don't be overly cocky or too pushy. Lead through example and not fear or intimidation. It is a good time to explore, do things you never did, ask for a raise, and put your foot down. However, remember that between September 9 and November 14, Mars is retrograde. Some delays and a pushback from life will take place. It might feel as if you are hitting the brakes after going 100 mph. Mars is traveling in your house of communication and relatives.

He gives you a boost of energy in study, writing, and socializing. However, he can create some challenges or a need to work with relatives and siblings.

Uranus - *Unpredictability, Originality, and a Touch of Chaos*

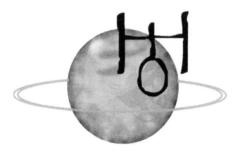

In March 2019, Uranus, your co-ruler, made his final move into Taurus, which is a square to your sign and not super-easy to channel. Uranus will remain in Taurus until 2026 and will be traveling in your house of home and family. Uranus is unpredictable and can create sudden disruptions and / or changes on your home front, either through some change in real estate or with a family member. Since Uranus is now transiting at the bottom of your chart, he is making adjustments to your foundation, to your emotional core. There could be some childhood memories that resurface as well as friends from your past that come back into your life. If you always wanted to change location, change a country or a city, this is not a bad time to use the Uranus energy to make that move.

Since Uranus is the Joker and Fool, someone in your family might act out of character or do something "crazy." Uranus is not a good or bad planet. He is associated with a powerful awakening, a leap of faith, and a jump into a new reality. You can use his energy to make emotional and physical changes and break away from ancestral karma, familial patterns, or whatever holds you back. Remember, as an Aquarius you have extra points with Uranus.

Uranus favors technology, innovation, and science. Maybe you can think of a great new application or an e-commerce business idea. It is also a good time to redo your website, give your Facebook page a face lift, and connect to social media. It is a good time to add technology to your home, maybe make it "smart" or green.

Your Hebrew Letter and Tarot Card:

Since 2020 is the year of 22, below is the Major Arcana card associated with your sign as well as the Hebrew letter. You can use the letter and place it inside the diamond in your meditation. The letter can also be used like a talisman to help you connect to your archetype. You will notice that in many cases, the letter's shape resembles its meaning. In my book *Cosmic Navigator*, you can find more information about the connection between the Hebrew letters and the zodiac signs.

Tarot: THE STAR

Hebrew letter: Tzadik

The letter means "a saint." The letter's shape resembles a fisherman, sitting holding a rod, catching fish. The fish is a metaphor for intuition and the Kabbalistic meaning of the letter is: meditation. Aquarius is the sign of altruism and selflessness. All they have to do is "fish" for the saint that is swimming inside of them.

Summary:

In 2020, you are called to use all you have learned in your life as an Aquarius and exercise your altruism, kindness, and love for humanity. The success of the year on all levels depends on your ability to let go, break patterns, and say "No!" to things that block you or keep you in chains. This year, you are beginning a new cycle that can help you become a completely new and upgraded version of yourself.

.

PISCES

New Karmic Cycle:
Let my People Go!

Since the end of 2017, you have been searching for your people, your tribe, your true friends and community — a fish looking for your school. This year, in addition to the process of letting go of the wrong people, companies, and communities, you can start discovering your true friendships. The last two years were filled with questions: who are my people? Where do I belong? Where is my tribe? Who can I influence and who can inspire me? Now, Jupiter is entering the scene with answers and opportunities to finally find the friends and fellowship you have longed for. Some of you will change companies, your circle of friends, and even move to a different city or country. In the first month of the year, you will be able to start a new cycle that will last a generation and help you connect with the right people. Since you have so many planets in the house of wishes and hopes, you will be able to manifest your dreams with much more ease. The question will be whether what you want is truly what you need. If they are one and the same, you can expect a great deal of universal help to you and your projects especially if they involve working with your friends or people you like. 2020 is the year you need to go out and make new acquaintances, connect to new clubs and organizations, even enter politics.

Between mid-March and the beginning of July, Saturn will briefly enter your house of letting go and past lives where it will also transit throughout 2021-2022. This is similar to what you experienced in 1991-1993 and it will be good to go back and see what lessons you downloaded then. Saturn in the house of letting go will connect you to dreams, imagination, and memories from past lives, but it is also associated with breaking patterns, hospitals, and separations. You will have to be a bit more careful from March to July and make sure you balance your health and mood swings. However, it is a good time to let go of whatever holds you back or blocks you.

In 2020 you will also have many opportunities to focus on your home, family, real estate, and perhaps relocate, especially when Venus visits your house of home between April and early August.

Since the eclipses are moving from the house of children to the house of home in June, this may manifest as a child coming into your family, buying a property, or changing location.

In the last six months of the year, you will find yourself with Mars traveling in your house of money. It is a good time to push your projects forward. Just make sure not to start anything new while Mars is retrograde (September 9 – November 14). Since Mars can be impulsive and impetuous, make sure not to make frivolous investments or purchases. You will have to fight for your rights from July through December and prove to yourself and everyone around you that you deserve respect, recognition, and financial compensation for your talents. Since Uranus is in your house of business, writing, and communication, you will have a great deal of unpredictable and unexpected changes in contracts and business. You are a mutable sign, so you know how to handle change very well. This position of Uranus can make you hilarious and ingenious. It is as if Uranus is enhancing your your IQ at least for the next few years.

The Six Eclipses
Your Emotional Landscape

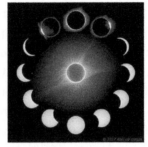

In Part I, I shared the meaning behind the eclipses and
their Sabian symbols and paths. To make it easier, I have
included some of that information below, as well as the
way the eclipses manifest in your sign.

Since January 2019, the eclipses have been in your house
of children, love, and creativity. The process of bringing
new love, new projects, babies, and new ideas into life
has quickened. The North Node in Cancer and Capricorn
were very helpful and easy for you to handle. However,
from June 2020 until the end of 2021, the eclipses are
shifting into Gemini, which is square to your sign. This
means that around the time of the eclipses, you will be
prompted into actions you might not feel comfortable
with, or are against your nature. You can go back to 2001
and 2002 and reflect on what manifested in your life
then.

Jan 10 / 11: Penumbral Lunar eclipse in Cancer. Sabian
symbol: Prima donna singing. Eclipse path: Europe,
Asia, Australia, Africa, most of North America, east part
of South America, Pacific, Atlantic, and Indian Oceans.

To understand the story of this eclipse, let's return to the movie analogy. The first act of your story took place during the eclipses of July 2019. The eclipse on January 10, 2020, is the second act of your film. The third and final act is performed on the eclipse of July 5, 2020. Pay attention to synchronicities or anything out of the ordinary taking place during these dates and try to link the events of the eclipses to a narrative. The eclipses fall in your house of children and love. You will feel an opposition between your need to connect to your children and your creativity versus the needs and wants of your friends or company. It is important to remember that the priority lies with your children and happiness.

June 5 / 6: Penumbral Lunar eclipse in Sagittarius.
Sabian symbol: Seagulls watching a ship. Eclipse path: Europe, most of Asia, Australia, Africa, south / east South America, Pacific, Atlantic, Indian Oceans. This eclipse is the first of the new Gemini-Sagittarius axial eclipses which will create a bit of a push-pull between home and family versus duty and career for the next 18 months. The Dragon favors your affiliation to your home and emotional well-being.

June 21: Solar Annular Solstice eclipse in Cancer.
Sabian symbol: A sailor ready to hoist a new flag to replace an old one. Eclipse path: south / east Europe, most of Asia, north Australia, most of Africa, Pacific and Indian Ocean. In addition, this eclipse takes place during a retrograde bonanza: Mercury, Venus, Pluto, Saturn, Pallas, and Jupiter are all in retrograde motion. This

means their expression is more internal and it will feel like you are a passenger in a car driven by a very bad driver. Take extra care of how you talk to and relate with lovers, friends, and authority figures. This eclipse is a good time to get pregnant or to start a new creative project. If you are single, it can manifest as a new love interest or a new sport or hobby.

July 4 / 5: Penumbral Lunar eclipse in Capricorn. Sabian symbol: An ancient bas-relief carved in granite. Eclipse path: south / west Europe, most of Africa, North America, South America, Pacific, Atlantic, and Indian Oceans. This eclipse is the mirror image of the Lunar eclipse of January 10 and therefore is the climax of whatever started for you in July 2019. Mercury is retrograde during this eclipse, therefore, we are still in danger of miscommunication and regretting our actions and / or choices. Again, you find yourself stuck between a lover and a friend, or your creativity and the demands of your company. Remember not to lose yourself in your loyalty to your company or friends but to be true to your love, children, and happiness.

Nov 29 / 30: Penumbral Lunar eclipse in Gemini. Sabian symbol: Quiver filled with arrows. Eclipse path: Europe, most of Asia, Australia, North America, South America, Pacific and Atlantic Oceans. The eclipse continues the exploration of what is true and what is false. It is a time to change the way we learn and teach. There could be a change of location because of a change in career or change of career because of a change of location.

Dec 14: Total Solar eclipse in Sagittarius. Sabian symbol: Blue bird standing at the door of the house. Eclipse path: South Africa, South America, Pacific, Atlantic, Indian Oceans. This is a powerful eclipse that begins a new journey in education, travel, and publishing. You might encounter an inspiring mentor or become one for someone else. This eclipse can bring about a new opportunity in your career, a raise or promotion, or a completely new path in your professional life.

Mercury Retrograde - *The Trickster*

Mercury is the trickster. Even when he is cruising direct through the heavens, he likes to pull practical jokes. I always thought that this was his compensation for delivering messages. When Mercury is retrograde, his tricks and ruses go to the next level. Of course, Mercury does not really retrograde, but from an earthly vantage point, Mercury does look as if he is going backwards three or four times a year for about three weeks. Mercury, the messenger of the gods and goddesses, represents the archetype of communication, connections, computers, emails, texts, messages, directions, information, data, cables, Wi-Fi, the nervous system, and breathing. During Mercury retrograde, all these aspects of life are reversed, malfunctioning. Error messages, delays, accidents, mishaps, misspelling, and glitches plague the earth.

During Mercury retrograde, it is not recommended to start new long-term projects, sign documents, make large purchases, get married, start marketing campaigns, publish, inaugurate locations or homes, or release new products. Communications of all sorts are slower and more challenging. Computers crash; stock markets turn volatile; flights are delayed; traffic is worse than usual; accidents occur more often; and Murphy's Law takes hold of all aspects of our lives. If you need to fly during Mercury retrograde, make sure you do your online check-in and allow more time to reach the airport. Try to avoid overscheduling yourself or being overly critical and demanding. Also pay attention to your diet and food intake.

If you must start a new project, be as mindful as you can. Pay attention to small details and read in-between the lines if you must sign a document. Rewrite your emails; edit your texts; and think before you speak or post. In fact, it is better if you spend more time listening than talking. Life does not come to a halt during Mercury retrograde. You can still achieve a great deal during his retrograde. It is like going on a vacation in Sweden in the winter: It can still be fun, just make sure you take a coat. However, Mercury retrograde is a great time to edit, redo, reexamine yourself and your path, revisit old projects, and find lost objects. Try to focus on activities that have the prefix *re* – reevaluate, reedit, redo, reexamine, reconnect, regenerate, revisit, re-imagine, etc.

Mercury is a liminal god and also a shadow-walker, a psychopomp, and a wizard (Hermetic studies are named after his Greek name). Jung identified him as the god of synchronicities, and it is true that during Mercury retrograde there are far more synchronicities and meaningful coincidences. Yes, you might have made it to the wrong place for your meeting, but there you bump into someone you have been unable to track for ages. And yes, you might arrive to the appointment at 9 AM instead of 9 PM, but because of that "mistake," you may have avoided a terrible accident.

You and Mercury don't always see eye-to-eye. In fact, when Mercury is in your sign, he is called "detriment," which is not a nice thing to call the planet of intelligence. Sometimes you and Mercury are like water (Pisces) on laptops (Mercury). Your high EQ does not always fit well with Mercury's interest in IQ. However, this year, the retrogrades are taking place in water signs, which could help ease some of the tension. Especially pay attention from February 16 – March 10, when Mercury is retrograde in your sign.

1st Retro: February 16 – March 10. From Feb 16 to March 4 Mercury is retrograde in Pisces which is your house of body and personality. Since it is your sign, watch your health and how you present yourself to others. There may be a great deal of confusion around first impressions and your identity.

From March 4 to March 10, Mercury is retrograde in Aquarius — your house of letting go, pain, and suffering. Yes, I know it sounds bad. Be careful of relapsing into old patterns or addictions. There is a little more tendency for self-destruction than usual.

2nd Retro: June 18 – July 12. Mercury retrogrades in Cancer. Be careful with this one, since it takes place during the powerful eclipse on June 21st. This retrograde is in your house of children and love; there could be miscommunication with lovers and children, or around creative projects.

3rd Retro: Oct 13 – Nov 3. Mercury is retrograde in Scorpio between October 13 and October 28, when Mars is also retrograde. This double retro motion also happened in July and August 2018. You can look back to that time, see what happened and maybe avoid similar mistakes. If you work with foreigners or travel, pay extra attention to small glitches and lack of organization during this time. If you are teaching or studying, be extra aware of your communication and writing. From October 28 to November 3 Mercury will be retrograde in Libra, which may be intense as this is your house of death, sexuality, investments, and intimacy. Do not make any investments during this retrograde.

Venus
Love, Pleasure, Art and Finance

Everyone loves Venus. Actually, what I just wrote, to an ancient Greek, would sound like a redundancy, since Venus embodies love and who does not love *love*?
But this year, it will be harder to love love, since Venus will be retrograding in Gemini between May 13 to June 25. She will be riding the Dragon, North Node, like an angry Khaleesi, who was just rejected by her John Snow. Venus goes retrograde once in 18 months for 40 days and 40 nights. It is a time we should dedicate to reevaluating our relationships, what we attract and what we are attracted to, how we relate to others, what talents we use to make money, as well as our core values and creeds. Some of us will have to confront insecurities and lower self-esteem during the retrograde. Many people change their attitudes, ideals, ethics, public image, dress code, and philosophies. It is a good time to get out of contracts that are not good for you.
Venus retrograde is a time when people are more blunt, combative, and lack diplomacy. You will also see a great deal of awkwardness on the world stage between diplomats as well as in the court system.

When Venus is retrograde, it is not recommended to get engaged or married, form business partnerships, buy art, make investments, start lawsuits, or spend money. If you are planning a cosmetic operation or an IVF, better wait for Venus to forget about her rejection and land her dragon safely on greener pastures.

Venus retrograde in Gemini specifically deals with how we communicate to our significant others, as well as relationships with business partners, siblings, and relatives. During Venus' long journey in Gemini (April 3 to August 7), we have the opportunity to connect beauty, art and finance with communication, technology, and business. Letters merge with notes, numbers with colors. Your art can be communicative and your communication artistic.

The retrograde can bring back money owed to you and reconnect you with a talent or a project that you have neglected from the past. You might also reconnect to a close friend from school.

Because of her retrograde motion, Venus will spend April to early August in your house of home and family. This presents a double-edged sword for you. On one side, having Venus bless your home can bring about a successful remodeling, or peace and harmony with family members, as well as an opportunity to invest in real estate (except between May 13 – June 25). However, Venus in Gemini is squaring your Sun and that can create challenges in partnerships, or overspending, or a tendency to live beyond your means. If you are a parent, be extra careful not to spoil or overindulge your children.

From January 13 to February 7, Venus transits in your sign. When Venus is in Pisces, she is considered exalted, meaning she is channeling her beauty and benevolence without hindrance. It is a good time to connect to your artistic talents and maybe have a boost in your income. When Venus is in your sign you feel attractive, artistic, and be glamourous. People are attracted to you and want to be next to you. Just be careful of being vain or overindulgent with food, spending, or drugs.

Mars
Assertion, Passion, Leadership

Mars is the engine of the zodiac. He is hot, driven, passionate, aggressive, explosive, and impulsive. The Romans saw him as their father and some scholars trace his mythological origins as a god of vegetation. Mars is still associated with spring and seeds. Even in Genesis 1:12, we find a hint of the connection between Mars and vegetation. On the third day of creation, that is on "Martes" (day of Mars), God created vegetation and seeds: "Let the earth burst forth with every sort of grass and seed-bearing plant, and fruit trees with seeds inside the fruit, so that these seeds will produce the kinds of plants and fruits they came from." And so it was, and God was pleased.

Between June 28 and the end of the year, Mars will be traveling in Aries. This is abnormal as usually Mars spends about six weeks, not six months, in a sign. Mars, the god of war, is the ruler of Aries, the sign of warfare. Yes, this can raise the probability of armed conflict, cyber-attacks, and other displays of aggression. This transit indicates there will be a great deal of strife, discord, and conflict. Astrology, like anything else in life is relative — you might feel more belligerent than your usual self. Call it an Incredible-Hulk aspect: things, people, and situations will drive you MADDDDDD!

This year, Mars will be retrograde in Aries between September 9 to November 14. When Mars is retrograding, it is not a very auspicious time to start big projects with large investments. It is not a good time for surgery and medical procedures unless urgent. Neither is it recommended to start an intimate or sexual relationship. Avoid buying big machinery, making large investments, or starting wars or lawsuits. It is a more dangerous time, since wars, conflicts, explosions, and terror seem to follow Mars. After all, Mars' moons are called Phobos (fear) and Deimos (terror). If you need to fight, let the opponent fire the first bullet. Whoever starts a war with Mars retrograde, loses.

The Brexit referendum took place during Mars retrograde in Aquarius, the sign of government and community.

And what happened right after? Oops, regret. What have we done? That is a typical Mars retrograde reaction. Another infamous example is the non-aggression treaty signed by Nazi Germany and the Soviets before WWII (Molotov-Ribbentrop), It was also a Mars retrograde station, and, obviously did not last long. Even though Mars retrograde is not the same as a Mercury retrograde, best to avoid signing treaty or agreements that deal with action, wars, or campaigns. Be mindful of what you agree to do, what you promise to carry out, what you fight for, and what you are willing to do to satiate your passions. Mars retrograde is a good time to review your past strategies, rethink your battles and wars, change direction in leadership, and admit that you were wrong. Take extra care between October 13 and November 4, since both Mars and Mercury are retrograde. Miscommunications and misunderstandings can easily flare into full-fledged wars.

Below is a list of Mars transits through the signs that can help you determine where to focus your energy. However, remember that even the best fighters need a general. Make sure you pace yourself and control your inner warrior.

January 3 to February 16 – Mars in Sagittarius: This Mars transit gives you a good start of the year with energy and passion for travel, study, and authenticity. Mars in your house of career can bring you a boost in your professional life. There is a call for action, a need to assume a role of a leader and an initiator. However, be careful not to get over-excited and get into trouble with bosses or superiors. There is competition around you; choose your battles wisely.

February 16 to March 30 – Mars in Capricorn: Mars through the filter of Capricorn exhibits his best qualities. He is the trained martial artist, fighting only when it is needed and he can easily win. However, be aware that Mercury retrograde might slow things down. Mars is in your house of friends, government, and organization. It is a powerful position for Mars in your chart as you are the sign of friends and community. It means you might be called to a leadership position, but watch for pointless conflicts and aggression with friends. Try not to be reactive.

March 30 to May 13 – Mars in Aquarius: This is a good time to fight for your ideals, for your group and company, and come to the rescue of a friend in need. However, it can also create conflict with certain friends or people in your company. Mars in the house of hospitals and retreat might manifest as a feeling of tiredness and sadness. However, this position favors meditation, dance, yoga, and any active mystical engagement. You might have some prophetic dreams. Act on your intuition!

May 13 to June 28 – Mars in Pisces: With this transit of Mars, you have to make sure you are getting enough sleep and rest.

Give time for your immune system to recover. It is a good time for interval fasting as well as for meditation and yoga. Two powerful eclipses, as well as Venus retrograde, are taking place and it can be intense out there. It is a good time for physical activities near or in water such as swimming, surfing, rowing, hiking / running / cycling by a body of water. Mars in your sign adds a great deal of intensity to this already intense year. This is a call to action, the need for a new adventure. Mars is helping you make decisions and take action. Be careful not to overstretch yourself or overstrain.

June 29 – End of the Year – Mars in Aries: Mars likes to be home in Aries, the sign of his rulership. The king is back in his palace. However, it can get hot and aggressive. Mars in Aries can be domineering — so back off and don't be overly cocky or too pushy. Lead through example and not with fear or intimidation. It is a good time to explore, do things you have never done, ask for a raise, and put your foot down. However, remember that between September 9 and November 14, Mars is retrograde. Some delays and a pushback from life will take place. It might feel as if you are hitting the brakes after going 100 mph. Mars is traveling in your house of money, talents, and self-worth. Be careful not to be too impulsive or overconfident with your finances. This retrograde can create situations where you will feel that money is slipping through your fingers. So be extra careful.

Uranus - *Unpredictability, Originality, and a Touch of Chaos*

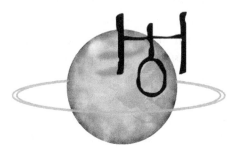

In March 2019, Uranus, the Joker and Fool, moved into your house of communication, contracts, relatives, and writing and will remain there until 2026. You might find yourself expressing yourself in a funnier way, becoming the standup comedian in your circle of friends. Your writing and communication skills will improve, even though they might be more erratic and spontaneous. Uranus is ingenious and original; this is a time to try to think of new ideas for businesses or commerce, especially if it involves technology, innovation, e-commerce, or anything that is out of the box. The more original you are, the more success is promised. Relationships with neighbors or relatives could go through a roller-coaster with a great deal of sudden twists and turns. But Uranus, being the great awakener, might create the groundwork for working with people you consider your brothers and sisters, even if you do not share your genes. Uranus favors technology, innovation, and science. Maybe you can think of a great new application, patent, or e-commerce business idea. It is also a good time to redo your website, give your Facebook page a face lift, and connect to social media.

Your Hebrew Letter and Tarot Card:

Since 2020 is the year of 22, below is the Major Arcana card associated with your sign as well as the Hebrew letter. You can use the letter and place it inside the diamond in your meditation. The letter can also be used like a talisman to help you connect to your archetype. You will notice that in many cases, the letter's shape resembles its meaning. In my book *Cosmic Navigator*, you can find more information about the connection between the Hebrew letters and the zodiac signs.

Tarot: THE MOON

Hebrew letter: Kuf

ק

The letter means "back of the head." The letter's shape resembles a head in profile and the spinal cord. Pisces is the sign of imagination and we now know that imagination flows from the parietal to the occipital centers, both located in the back of the head.

Summary:

2020 is an intense year and it mainly focuses on changing or consolidating your tribe, company, or people you consider your friends, fans, or clients. In the second part of the year, your focus will change to improving your financial situation and fighting for your values, as well as a need to build your home and create a family.

Made in the USA
Middletown, DE
19 November 2019